ISBN: 9781290472692

Published by:
HardPress Publishing
8345 NW 66TH ST #2561
MIAMI FL 33166-2626

Email: info@hardpress.net
Web: http://www.hardpress.net

THE LIGHTER SIDE OF MY OFFICIAL LIFE

THE LIGHTER SIDE OF MY OFFICIAL LIFE

BY SIR ROBERT ANDERSON
K.C.B., LL.D.

HODDER AND STOUGHTON
NEW YORK AND LONDON

PREFACE

A BOOK of this kind needs no preface, save to express the author's acknowledgments to Messrs. William Blackwood and Sons for sanctioning the republication of articles which recently appeared in *Blackwood's Magazine*.

If, notwithstanding the author's estimate of these articles, as indicated in his opening sentences, he now reissues them in book form, he does so in response to appeals from many quarters. It has been pressed upon him, moreover, that they must be of exceptional interest, seeing that they were made the subject of "a full-dress debate" in Parliament; and that, too, at a time when opportunity could not be found for any adequate discussion of great questions of national importance and gravity.

CONTENTS

CHAPTER I

CHAPTER II

CHAPTER III

Contents

Contents

CHAPTER I

Scheme of the book—Some personal details—French versions of nursery rhymes—Life in Trinity College, Dublin — " The Irish Question ": Lord Morris's definition of it—The College Historical Society—A mock criminal trial—The Irish Bench and Bar, reminiscences and incidents—The Fenian trials in Ireland and in England contrasted.

EVEN in the case of people of distinction an autobiography is too often a blunder. In the case of commonplace folk it is generally an impertinence. And I am not so foolish as to suppose that the public would care to know anything about me save in relation to matters of public interest. Here, however, I am in a difficulty. Having regard to the position I held for so long at Whitehall, and in more recent times at Scotland Yard, I cannot even now write about the Secret Service, or police work in London, save with much reserve and under definite restraints. But it is constantly urged upon me that even the lighter side of official life in these spheres has a fascination for many people, and that I might say not a little which would interest and amuse the public; and it is with this modest aim therefore that, postponing graver "reminiscences" to a future date, I now take up my pen.

By way of introduction I may describe myself as an Anglicanised Irishman of Scotch extraction. My "forebears" were among the Scotch colonists who made Ulster what it is. My only further reference to family history will be to mention that an ancestor of my mother, and an ancestor of my wife's mother, won fame in the siege of Derry—Colonel Gardner in command of royal troops, and Samuel Lee as leader of the "Prentice Boys," the freemen of Derry, to whom the sustained defence of the maiden city was chiefly due. Born and bred in Dublin, my home life in Ireland was interrupted only by two years spent in France—one year in Boulogne and one in Paris. In view of recent events in France, certain reminiscences of my school days in Boulogne are not without interest. It was then the habit of the children of the lower orders to insult the priests, a practice which indicated the sort of influence that prevailed in their homes. And we English boys fared still worse at their hands. *Corbeau* was the usual epithet shouted after a priest as he passed along the street; *Sale Anglais, Vaterloo*, was the signal for many a scrimmage in which we had to stand on our defence, or not infrequently, I must confess, to bolt.

Of my life in Paris I will not speak, though if I were somebody else about whom I might speak in the third person I should be tempted to téll something of what a schoolboy saw and heard in the French capital in the early days of the Second Empire. And not a little of the chatter of my French playmates might possibly be worth repeating—as, *ex. gr.*, the versions they gave me of some of our English rhymes. Never since have I heard them, nor have I ever seen them in print. Here is a specimen—

"Petit bo-bouton
A perdu ses moutons,
Et ne sait pas qui les a pris.
O laissez les tranquilles,
Ils viendront en ville,
Et chacun son queue après lui."

And our old friend Humpty Dumpty is better still—

"Umpety Dumpety pendait au mur,
Umpety Dumpety tombait si dur,
Ni tous les chevaux ni les hommes du roi
Mettraient Umpety Dumpety comme autrefois."

But I am forgetting the self-denying ordinance paraded on my opening page.

My Official Life

When I left school, a rich and sonless friend of my father, the owner of one of the famous Dublin breweries, brought me into his business with the generous intention of making my fortune. And I may mention with pardonable pride that within a year I was promoted to be cashier in this great commercial house. But the love of money does not become a passion in the schoolboy stage of life; and after eighteen months in the office I became increasingly conscious of my deficiencies in "book-learned skill," to borrow Goldsmith's phrase. A Dublin University degree might be obtained without residence, by passing the prescribed examinations, and I appealed to my would-be benefactor to consent to my absenting myself from the office on all examination days. But this he refused, and his refusal led to my abandoning "business." And four years later I was called to the Irish Bar.

I cherish pleasant memories of those years. Religion and politics are the bane of Ireland. But the politicians and the priests had not yet poisoned the life of the country: and in Trinity College Orangemen and Romanists, "ferocious Radicals" and high Tories, mixed together and discussed their differences with the courtesy and kindliness of Irish gentlemen. We learned to give and take, and to respect one another’s opinions. This element has always been characteristic of Trinity College, and it is precisely the element which evokes the implacable hostility of Maynooth. There may perhaps be two sides to the Home Rule controversy; and it is possible that if Home Rule had been granted half a century ago it might have proved a success. But there are no two sides to this University question. And the men who are responsible for setting up a University designed to keep Irishmen apart, and to teach them to distrust or despise those who differ from them in religion, will deserve to be pilloried for all time. No greater evil could be inflicted on that unfortunate country. Among “the benefits of a University education” one of the greatest is precisely the element which a sectarian University is intended to eliminate.

But *cui bono?* At a certain stage of life people are apt to become slovenly-minded. They “don’t want to be bothered.” And this is the attitude which England seems now to adopt toward Irish questions. In the scramble for office a philosopher is appointed to govern Ireland. He is followed by a Chief Secretary who belongs (shall I say?) to a different category. In due course the country is naturally reduced to a condition of utter lawlessness and demoralisation. And what is to be done? The row in the nursery is intolerable: the children are quarrelling and screaming because they cannot get this or that. "Well, let them have whatever they want. We can't have this disgraceful noise." In this parable lies "the Irish question." Lord Morris' witty definition of it applies with special aptness to-day. "It was," he said, "the attempt of an honest, stupid people to govern a quick-witted, dishonest people." And this *mot* applies not only to the two nations but to the men who respectively represent them on the front bench and below the gangway of the House of Commons.

While all my memories of Trinity College are pleasant, the pleasantest are those which relate to the clubs and societies, and first and chiefest to the famous "College Historical"—sister society to the Unions of Oxford and Cambridge. The most distinguished members of the Society were my seniors,[1] but as my brother was their contemporary I was admitted to the circle of their friendship.

In the Historical Society it was that I acquired

[1] Not a few of them have since made their mark in the world. I may mention among others Lecky (the historian), Gibson (now Lord Ashbourne), Plunket (now Lord Rathmore), Wilson (now Rt. Hon. Sir Arthur Wilson, K.C.I.E.), and my friend from childhood's days, the late Lord Justice Fitzgibbon.

any little capacity I possess for public speaking. If, instead of being an utter sceptic, I were credulous enough to accept the biological theories of Spencer and Huxley, I should conclude that the particular "germ" from which my stock was evolved must have wriggled into life at a very late stage of evolutionary processes. For with us the gift of speech is as yet but imperfectly developed. From my father I inherited a natural inaptitude for speaking in public. Well do I remember my first attempt at the "Historical." We met in the great dining-hall of the College. The debate was an important one: the attendance of both members and the public was unusually large, and some of our best speakers had preceded me. I was half sick with nervousness when I rose, and before I was many minutes on my legs the big gasolier, and the distinguished Don who occupied the chair, both began to gyrate round me. My knees began to give way and my head to spin. I could no longer see my notes, and I was on the point of collapsing on the floor, when as an expiring effort I emitted one of my elaborately prepared "impromptus." It evoked a laugh and a cheer. The effect was magical. In an instant the chairman and the gasolier got back into position; my eyes followed suit, my legs stiffened, and when I sat down

I was heartily congratulated on my "maiden speech."

I soon became one of the regular speakers at the weekly debates, and in due course I was elected Auditor (or President) of the Society. The moral of which is that a man can do what he makes up his mind to do. In the morning paper that lies before me as I write, I see a notice of a police charge against a dumb man for using bad language. It reminds me of an answer I once heard my brother give when asked whether he could play the violin: "I don't know," said he, "I never tried"!

My reminiscences of College days are all the happier because they are free from any element to which one need look back with distress or regret. And yet we did some wild things. One such may be worth telling. In those days "Chief Baron Nicholson's" mock court in the "Cider Cellars" was one of the stock amusements of London.[1] I forget who it was that suggested the scheme of getting up an entertainment of the kind; but it caught on, and was carried

[1] The "Chief Baron" was said to be a barrister who had gone off the rails in some way; an unfailing variety and humour marked his use of a phenomenal stock of legal lore and classical erudition. His assistants, who "practised" in his court, were men of the same type. The jury were always selected from the audience, their only fees being free drinks.

through with great success. Manor Courts were then in existence. A Manor Court had a civil jurisdiction akin to that of the County Courts when first established. And the judge was nominated by the Lord of the Manor. My father was at this time "Seneschal of the Manor of Mary's Abbey," an appointment which he owed to the friendship of Lady Harriet Cowper, the Earl of Blessington's daughter. She, when a school-girl, had been married to Count d'Orsay by her stepmother, the notorious Countess, and was then the wife of Mr. Spencer Cowper, from whom the King's Sandringham estate was afterwards purchased. We decided to make use of my father's court-house for our scheme. Accordingly my brother notified the court-keeper that there would be a special session of the Court on the evening we had fixed upon; and when we turned up everything was ready, not excepting the presence of a police-constable at the door.

One of our number, who has since attained to fame at the Bar and in Parliament—first in the Commons and later as a Peer—took his place on the bench in borrowed wig and gown; and a certain divinity student, who afterwards became an Archdeacon, was put upon his trial for an assault of a somewhat disreputable kind. The combination of lying and cunning in the evidence of the witnesses seemed true to the life, and the speeches were marked by eloquence, though not altogether by relevancy. The seats allotted to the public were fairly occupied, for an evening sitting and a criminal trial were unprecedented events. But when the proceedings resulted in the conviction of the accused, and the "Judge" announced that "before d-dealing with the prisoner he really must have a sm-oke," and proceeded to light a cigar, we could hold out no longer, and there was a wild roar of laughter. "In which," as the newspapers would say, "the prisoner heartily joined." The "public" suddenly realised that they had been fooled, and stampeded from the place.

It is characteristic of life in Ireland in those days that we were not taken to task for our escapade. It was never reported or noticed in any way. And the Seneschal of the Manor heard of it for the first time long years afterwards, as he sat by his fireside with his grandchildren playing about his knees.

I have spoken of the liberality and generosity of thought which prevailed in Trinity College. In my time the Roman Catholics at the Irish Bar were, with rare exceptions, Trinity College men, and the same characteristics marked our professional intercourse. In no society that I have ever entered have I known more freedom in the expression of opinion. Hard knocks were sometimes given and received, and there was no lack of banter on what might be deemed delicate ground; but we took and gave with perfect good-humour.

An incident occurs to me which may illustrate my meaning. At a time when the Papal problem was much in evidence I was sitting in court one day while R. Dowse, Q.C., afterwards a well-known figure in the House of Commons, was arguing a case before a bench of judges, the majority of whom were Catholics. One of their number, Judge Ball, who had already "outlived his usefulness," interrupted with the silly question "But what is a clerical error?" Sharp as a pistol-shot came back the answer, "The present position of the Pope in Rome, my lord!" Dowse was always his own *claque*, and his ringing laugh was joined in by every man in the court, not excepting Ball's colleagues on the Bench.

Another characteristic of those days was the freedom with which educated Catholics spoke of Maynooth priests. In his judgment in the celebrated Galway election petition of 1872, Mr. Justice Keogh used some very strong language about the conduct of the priests. In the Bar Library in Dublin, one day, Mr. (afterwards Lord) Morris was defending that judgment against the censures of some of his co-religionists. Said one of them: "But, Morris, you would never have called a parish priest 'an obscene monster'?" "I would not," he replied; "but that's only Keogh's poetry. I would have called him a filthy brute!"

This was typical. On the closing day of the Londonderry Assizes, in my last year at the Irish Bar, I dined with the Judges—Chief Justice Monahan and Chief Baron Pigot—both of whom were Catholics. I was sitting next the Chief Justice, and he asked me what had become of Blank, a "junior" of very plebeian appearance, tastes, and manners. The Chief Baron had consented to his being asked to dine with them on this their last night, but he was not to be found. I hinted that he was probably in company more suited to his proclivities and his morals. He repeated my words to the Chief Baron across the table, and then, turning to me, he added, "Wouldn't Blank have made a fine priest?"

And yet Monahan was a devout religionist. And I must add that a Protestant landlord fared badly in his court if sued by a Roman Catholic tenant with his priest to back him. In 1867 I was Counsel for Sir Roger Palmer in a case of this kind, with Dowse as my leader; and as soon as the plaintiff and the priest had given their evidence, he adjourned the case without hearing us or our witnesses, and turning to the jury, he remarked, "And, gentlemen, if they don't settle it we'll know how to deal with them." It was a case that would never have been brought into court but for Monahan's well-known proclivities; but I need not say we "settled" it!

But with him the priest's evidence was vital. In a similar case on a Southern circuit (I can't personally vouch for this story) "his Reverence," though freely quoted, was not called as a witness. Addressing the plaintiff's counsel by the pet name by which he was known to his intimates, Monahan exclaimed, "But, Davie, are you not going to call the priest?" And on receiving a reply in the negative he emitted a sound as nearly resembling a whistle as ever was heard from the Bench, and turning to the jury, he said with a nod, "Gentlemen, he won't call the priest." In that case there was a verdict for the defendant.

Monahan was utterly unconventional. One of his sons was his registrar, and he usually addressed him by his Christian name in open court. Indeed, he always did so when scolding him. I remember once, when the registrar was swearing in a jury, and a well-known member of the Society of Friends failed to comply with the order to "take the book," twice repeated in a peremptory tone, the Chief Justice blurted out, D—n your soul, Harry! don't you see he's a Quaker?"

This digression, which has resulted from my reference to the Irish University question, would leave a false impression if I did not add that in those days we had great judges in Ireland, and great forensic orators and advocates; and trials were usually conducted with marked ability and with perfect fairness and dignity. Some modern English judges are in the habit of indulging in comments intended to be humorous in the progress of a case. But this would not be tolerated in Ireland. In my day, at least, a judge who thus played the part of the "bones" in a nigger minstrel troupe would have risked reprisals from the Bar. I recall an instance of the kind. It was an action against a Turkish bath company by a man who fainted in the hot room of the bath, and got badly burnt. "I'll not go there to be burned," the judge exclaimed, while the plaintiff was giving his evidence. "No, my lord, you'll wait!" was the immediate rejoinder of my friend Dowse, who led for the defendants; and everybody in court roared with laughter at the judge's expense. There were no more "bones" interruptions that day.

Monahan himself was an admirable judge in any case that did not excite his well-known prejudices. Magna Charta precludes the King from delaying justice; but what the King may not do, judges do habitually by spinning out trials and wantonly granting adjournments that involve the unfortunate litigants in great inconvenience and expense. Monahan had a highly developed faculty for getting at the facts of a case; and in his court a few hours sufficed for a trial over which his friend the Chief Baron would have spent as many days. And as regards criminal procedure, we had nothing to learn from England. The Fenian trials which followed the outrages at Manchester and Clerkenwell in 1867 contrasted very unfavourably with the State trials in Dublin earlier in that year. Of course the Irish prisoners declaimed against England and English law, but one and all they admitted the fairness with which they had been tried, whereas the Manchester trial was discredited by the conviction of a man who was afterwards proved to be innocent, and the conduct of the Clerkenwell case was marked by still greater incompetence.

As I have told elsewhere, Chief Justice Cockburn was so dissatisfied with it that if I had not been able to relieve his doubts when he came to the Home Office to discuss the question of a reprieve, even Barrett would have escaped the gallows.

That Clerkenwell hanging has historic interest, by the way, as being the last public execution in this country. At Edmund Yates's dinner-table I had a most animated account of it from him and J. C. Parkinson, both of whom were present as journalists on the occasion.

CHAPTER II

Entrance into Government work—The "Fenian Rising" and the "Clerkenwell explosion" of 1867—Panic caused in London: illustrative incidents—Interview with a clairvoyant informant of Lord Derby's—The Birdcage Walk mystery of January, 1868: panic in London.

IN my Irish book[1] I have explained how it came about that I was called in to assist at Dublin Castle in 1867. The early years of a barrister's career are often a time of anxious and weary waiting for briefs. But I belonged to the favoured and fortunate class who become self-supporting from the very start. And though I was not professionally employed at the State trials of 1865, I had access, not only to the Crown briefs, but to the information which led to the prosecutions of that year. When, therefore, on

[1] "Sidelights on the Home Rule Movement." The Library Edition of this book is out of print. But an abridged sixpenny edition, under the title "A Great Conspiracy," has been published by Mr. John Murray.

his coming into office in 1866, Lord Mayo sought for some one to coach him about Fenianism, my name was put before him by the Under Secretary, and I was commissioned to make a *précis* of all the secret and confidential papers which had reached the Government relating to the Fenians, both at home and in the United States. And having completed my task, I proceeded to write a history of the Fenian conspiracy up to date, which proved of value to the Government. This again led to my services being requisitioned by the Attorney-General when "the Fenian Rising" occurred in March, 1867. In the autumn of that year I was for the third time called in to advise and assist at Dublin Castle; and I was thus engaged when the Clerkenwell explosion took place in December.

I must not forget that these pages will be read by a generation of men who have grown to manhood since that event occurred, and for their benefit a brief account of it may be opportune.

A prominent Irish-American Fenian, Ricard Burke by name, who had been for some time 'arms agent" to the conspirators, fell into the hands of the police in November, 1867, and was committed to the House of Detention at Clerkenwell. This miscreant hatched a plot for the rescue of himself and another Fenian who was his fellow-prisoner. In Dublin we received full particulars of the project, and in due course the information was given to the Home Office and to the authorities at Scotland Yard. The following is an extract from this warning notice, as afterwards communicated to the House of Commons by the Secretary of State:

"The rescue of Ricard Burke from prison in London is contemplated. The plan is to blow up the exercise walls by means of gunpowder; the hour between 3 and 4 p.m.; and the signal for 'all right,' a white ball thrown up outside when he is at exercise."

On December 12th, at the hour named, the police on duty outside the prison witnessed a rehearsal of the plot. A cask of gunpowder was conveyed to the place on a truck, and before a light was put to the fuse a white ball was thrown over the wall into the exercise-ground as a warning to Burke. He immediately "fell out" on pretence of having a stone in his shoe, and sought safety in a remote corner of the yard. But the fuse was damp, and failed to explode the powder.

So the whole performance was repeated next day, and again under the watchful eyes of the police. The barrel of powder was rolled to the same spot, and the white-ball signal was given as before, and the explosion followed. The prison authorities took the precaution of exercising the prisoners in a different yard, but the police took no action of any kind. The Commissioner of Police, Sir Richard Mayne, freely acknowledged that their conduct was inexcusable, and he was never the same man again. On my first visit to the Home Office I learned that he had at once placed his resignation in the hands of the Secretary of State, but Mr. Hardy refused to accept it. As Mr. Liddell, the Under-Secretary, put it in his characteristic way, "We told him he had made a —— fool of himself, but we meant to pull him through; we weren't going to throw him over after his long public service."

The explanation of this, offered by the Secretary of State in Parliament (March 9, 1868), reads more like a Mark Twain story than a Hansard report. It was to the effect that the police were misled by the terms of the warning. It said the wall was to be blown up, whereas in fact it was blown down! Here are Mr. Hardy's words:—

"It appeared that the mode of carrying out the design of which they had received information did not strike those who were set to watch the outside of the prison. . . . What their attention was apparently directed to was the undermining of the wall; they thought it would probably be blown up from underneath, and had no conception that it would be blown down in the way it really was done."

It was an atrocious crime, and it would have served its purpose had Burke been in the coign of safety to which he had retreated the preceding day. But if the yard had been occupied, he alone would have escaped serious injury. I was reminded of the condition of the opposite premises when, after the siege of Paris, I witnessed the effects of bombs upon dwelling-houses. Four persons were killed, and some forty others were carried to hospital, "suffering from all forms of mutilation." It was indeed a heinous and hideous crime. But, regarded with reference to a political conspiracy, it was contemptible. This needs to be said, lest the historian should perpetuate the false estimate of the outrage which prevailed at the time. Even the "Annual Register," which is supposed to furnish material for history, spoke of "the certainty that the explosion was planned by the American-Irish who managed the conspiracy." And it added:—

"Great vigilance was for some time required, and strict precautions were properly taken, to protect the public edifices and the places which were threatened with attack, or were peculiarly exposed to acts of wanton mischief; but the fact of the Government being thus forewarned and forearmed sufficed both to deter the conspirators from a further prosecution of their plots, and to reassure the peaceable and well-disposed part of the community of the protection of the law."

As a matter of fact, the Clerkenwell explosion was not the work of the Fenian organisation at all, but of a small gang of low-class London Irish within its ranks. At this time, moreover, the organisation had ceased to be formidable. In the beginning of 1867 Fenianism was a power to be reckoned with, both in the United Kingdom and in America; but the events of the year had utterly discredited the movement and demoralised the conspirators. The most ordinary police precautions would have prevented the outrage, and a competent Intelligence Department would have prevented the wild scare which the outrage produced.

The apathy which had prevailed till then gave place at once to unreasoning panic. The explosion occurred on a Friday. The Cabinet met next day and decided to adopt heroic measures to cope with what was supposed to be a great national crisis. On the Monday a Home Office circular called for the enrolment of special constables, and a body of over 50,000 was thus raised in London within the month, and more than double that number throughout the provinces.

Another project decreed by the Cabinet was the organisation temporarily of a Secret Service Department. To undertake this duty the Home Secretary nominated Colonel the Hon. William Feilding of the Guards, who had done good work in Ireland in checking the spread of Fenianism among the troops. Lord Mayo's choice fell on me, and I was invited to co-operate. When I came to London the following week, the scheme submitted to me was that we should take up our quarters in a private house in some quiet street and "work underground." To this I objected, not only for professional reasons, but because I believed that secrecy on such lines would be impossible. In Mexico, it is said, people speak the truth only when they wish to deceive; and a display of openness is always a good screen for secrecy. I would consent to remain only if attached to a Government Department. Lord Mayo took my view of the matter, and I was installed in the law room at the Irish Office. Colonel Feilding carried out the other project with the help of Captain Whelan of the 8th Regiment. They were both friends of mine, and the joint scheme worked admirably.

The panic which prevailed in London at this time was absolutely ludicrous. When I took up the *Times* on the morning of my arrival (December 19, 1867), I learned that, the night before, "a great number of detective police were sent out on duty into different parts of the city." And further, that "the South Kensington Museum, the British Museum, the gas factories, the powder magazines, &c., &c., were all protected by officers of the police and military." By every post Ministers received letters from panic-stricken folk, or from lunatics or cranks, reporting suspicious incidents, or giving warning of plots upon public or private property. And the "specials" had a bad time of it, doing "sentry-go" in the streets on foggy nights when they ought to have been in their beds.

My friendship with Montague Corry, afterwards Lord Rowton, dated from this time. When meeting him at the Home Office I persuaded him that it was quite unnecessary to carry a revolver. All the private secretaries carried arms, he told me. And the Fenians were credited with the intention, not only of murdering public officials, but of burning public buildings and private houses. Paragraphs and letters in the newspapers every day gave warning that "Fenian Fire," or "Greek Fire," as it was called, would be used for this purpose, and advising that, as water would not quench it, a supply of sand should be kept in readiness—advice which was acted on at Whitehall, if not elsewhere.

As a matter of fact, the Clerkenwell explosion frightened the Fenians quite as much as it frightened the Government. The wretched men who fired that fuse meant only to make a breach in the prison wall, and it never occurred to them that they would wreck the opposite houses. And though, as I have said, the Fenian leaders in London had no part in the outrage, they expected to suffer in consequence of it; and if sensible measures of repression had been adopted they would have submitted without a protest. But when they discovered that, by exploding a cask of gunpowder, they could throw not only the public but the Government of this country into hysterics, they rallied from their fright, and set themselves to profit by the lesson.

I suppose I ought to have accepted the situation and posed as the saviour of my country; but my efforts were chiefly aimed at preventing or exploding scares. In some quarters my cynical scepticism was not appreciated; but I had a powerful "backer" in Mr. Liddell, the Permanent Under-Secretary at the Home Office, a man who was the impersonation of sound judgment and common-sense.

The following characteristic incident may serve to illustrate the daily occurrences of this period. Lord Derby received a letter, evidently from a lady of culture, giving details of a serious Fenian plot to attack the Bank of England on a certain night. The writer added that it would not be convenient to her to see any one on the subject; nor would anything be gained by an interview, as she could add nothing to her written statement. But she implored the Prime Minister not to neglect the warning, as the quarter from which the information came was a guarantee of its value. This matter was deemed too serious to trust to special constables, and it was proposed to double the usual military guard at the Bank. I protested that by action of this kind we were reviving Fenianism and creating future trouble; and I sought and obtained Lord Derby's consent to my investigating the matter before any orders were issued.

That afternoon I set out upon my errand. The address given in the letter proved to be a lodging-house which had an unmistakably Irish name upon the door, and it occurred to me at once that the writer might have overheard what she narrated, and that her story might after all be important. Gaining admittance by a ruse and under an assumed name, I was shown into a room on the first floor, half boudoir, half bedroom. There I was received by a very charming elderly lady, who shook hands with me, saying, "You have come from Lord Derby?" "Lord Derby!" I exclaimed. "Do you mean the Prime Minister?" "Yes," said she with a smile, "you can't deceive me; I have ways of finding out things. I have no doubt you have my letter to Lord Derby in your pocket." With a laugh I assented, and proceeded to talk about the subject of my visit. But she insisted on talking about herself, in order, as she said, to satisfy me that she was deserving of trust. She gave me a sketch of her life, and showed me a number of letters from persons of distinction, in whose houses she had lived either as governess or companion—letters which gave proof that she was held by them in high esteem. Some forty minutes were spent in this way before I could lead her to the business I had in hand. She then lowered her voice and repeated to me the substance of her letter to the Prime Minister. I discussed the matter with her and tried in vain to induce her to disclose the source of her information. But at last her power of resistance gave way, and she told me that she was in the habit of receiving heavenly visions, and that this plot had been divinely revealed to her.

I was completely taken aback. Till then her whole manner and bearing had impressed me most favourably, and I was looking forward to apologising at headquarters for my dogmatism. But there was more to follow. Then and there she lapsed into some sort of trance, her eyes became fixed, and in a changed voice she described what was passing before her. I was held like the wedding-guest by the Ancient Mariner. To this day the incident lives in my memory. I will not attempt to explain it, but will only add that the Bank of England was never raided by the Fenians, nor was the military guard increased.

The "Clerkenwell explosion" was not the only London sensation of that winter. An event occurred some four weeks later which, in the language of the *Annual Register*, "occasioned an almost universal panic." On the afternoon of January 8th a Somersetshire clergyman arrived in London in order to officiate at a wedding. Leaving his portmanteau at the house of a relative in Pimlico, he announced that he had to go to Westminster on business, but would be back in an hour or so. Then he disappeared, and in the evening his hat was picked up in the Birdcage Walk. A wild scare resulted; for the inference seemed obvious that he had been either murdered or kidnapped. Not paragraphs merely, but leading articles on the case appeared in every newspaper. The prosaic *Times* had a couple, and the sedate *Spectator* became almost hysterical over it. "Twenty or thirty thousand minds," it declared, "have been at work upon the case, including the whole body of Police, the entire Bar, and the whole body of Clubmen" of the Metropolis. The scare was fomented by a letter to the *Times* of February 5th from the well-known chaplain of the Savoy. When passing through Trafalgar Square, he said, a cab drew up beside him, and the occupant, springing out, announced that the Chief Magistrate requested his immediate presence at Bow Street to give evidence in a pending case. Mr. White refused the man's urgent appeal to accompany him in the cab; and when he afterwards made his way to the Court he learned that the whole story was false. "A new form of crime has been invented, in which a confederate drives a cab," was the Press comment on the incident. Mr. White of the Savoy Chapel had narrowly escaped the same fate as the victim of the Birdcage Walk tragedy.

Six weeks after his disappearance, a man was arrested at Padstow, in Cornwall, on suspicion of being wanted for an offence committed at Hull. Though dressed as a bullock driver, his pocket contained more money than a bullock driver was likely to possess. Accordingly, he was remanded for inquiries ; and the inquiries resulted in finding a portmanteau containing several "disguises," and a diary which gave proof that he was not the Hull criminal but the missing parson.

CHAPTER III

From the Irish Office to the Home Office—Reminiscences of the House of Commons—Hearing H.M.'s speech on the opening of Parliament in 1861—Captain Gosset's friendship—"Gosset's Room": House of Commons stories—The House of Lords gallery—The *personnel* and ways of the Home Office forty years ago—The old Home Office and the new—Red tape at the Foreign Office and the War Office—A tribute to Sir Adolphus Liddell.

As already intimated, the Secret Service Department, which was organised in London after the Clerkenwell explosion, was intended to be temporary, and in fact it lasted only for three months. Though my sojourn in London had proved an interesting and enjoyable episode in my life, I was eagerly looking forward to returning to the Irish Bar, when I learned that the Government wished to retain my services at Whitehall. Mr. Gathorne Hardy invited me to take charge of Irish business at the Home Office, and Lord Mayo put pressure on me to comply.

I had an intelligent aversion to the Civil Service—an aversion which my experience of it has not quenched. And when asked to come to London I laid the matter before the Irish Attorney-General, and received his assurance that, so far from injuring my professional prospects, my mission would give me further claims upon him for preferment. And shortly afterwards he proved the sincerity of his words by appointing me to a Crown Prosecutorship on my circuit. I referred to him again, therefore, at this juncture; and again he urged me to undertake the duties required of me, telling me in confidence that he expected shortly to have in his gift a principal Prosecutorship on the circuit, and that I should be remembered in connection with it. This decided my course, and in April, 1868, I moved from the Irish Office to Whitehall.

But though Mr. Warren was one of the most honourable of men, his promise was not fulfilled. When the appointment in question became vacant, he wrote to me that he could not ignore pressure put upon him against recalling me to Ireland. For a typical Treasury letter had just been received remonstrating against the cost of retaining me in London; and on this letter Mr. Hardy had placed the laconic minute, "Mr. Anderson's services are indispensable." I decided, therefore, to remain at all events until I could get called to the English Bar.

I was not insensible, moreover, to the attractions of life in London. The House of Commons always had a special charm for me. Even in the days when I was a law student at the Temple, "the Lobby" attracted me more than evening entertainments of the kind frequented by my "pals." I used to make friends with the police on duty, and by their help I obtained Members' orders for the gallery. One of their number, who, by the way, was a fellow-countryman of mine, let me in for a unique experience.

How many living men are there, I wonder, other than M.P.'s, who have entered the House of Lords along with the "faithful Commons" to hear the Royal Speech at the opening of Parliament? My police constable friend put me up to this. "If we catch you" said he, "it's not in the House of Lords you'll find yourself; but we'll not catch you if you do what I tell you." I did what he told me In those pre-dynamite days there was no difficulty in getting into the Lobby; and on the 5th of February, 1861, I found myself in the middle of a group of M.P.'s who were waiting there. Presently the Speaker's stately procession to "the gilded Chamber" came along; and as soon as the leading Members had passed, the waiting group closed in with a rush. Had I been as anxious to keep out as I was to get in, nothing could have stopped me. I was carried almost off my feet, and it was not till I found myself inside the House of Lords that I was able even to raise my hand to get my hat off my head. Some of the Members were much amused at finding me in their midst, and quizzed me about my constituency. Donnybrook Fair had attracted the notice of Parliament at that time, because of the rowdyism which led to its abolition; and their amusement was increased when I told them I was M.P. for Donnybrook, and that my experience in the Lobby made me think myself back among my constituents.

After-events lent a special interest to that occasion. It was the last opening of Parliament at which "Her Majesty's own words" were heard from Her Majesty's own lips. For after the Prince Consort's death Queen Victoria never read her Speech in person.

When I returned to the Metropolis in 1868 the House of Commons had still greater attractions for me. My enjoyment of life in London at that time owed more than I can tell to the friendship of Captain Gosset, the Assistant Sergeant-at-Arms. I was always welcome at his dinner-table, and seldom a week passed that I did not avail myself of his hospitality—a real privilege to a bachelor living in London lodgings. But more than this, his friendship made me practically free of the Chamber. I was thus enabled to attend the historic debates of that memorable time when there were Parliamentary giants in the land, whose set speeches were classic orations of a type unknown to the present generation.

But this was not all. The majority of the M.P.'s of to-day never even heard of "Gosset's room." But in those days the Assistant Sergeant's office room was a notable institution. It was in fact a *quasi* social club. The etiquette which regulated it was strict. No one frequented the room without a definite invitation, but an invitation made a man free of it afterwards. It was situated in one of the inner corridors, and of course none but M.P.'s had access to it, the only exceptions being Captain Gosset's sons and one or two other immediate relatives, and myself. I was thus brought into touch with all the by-play of the House, and met the *élite* of its Members.

What a book I might write if only I had kept a note of the good things I heard there! These pages seem to be running on the lines of that type of sermon that consists of a series of theses with an illustrative incident for each. The following may serve for the present "thesis." A Mr. Pim, an Irish Quaker, and one of the most estimable and courteous of men, was returned at this time as M.P. for Dublin. Like many new Members, he was eager to hear, and being deaf, he used constantly to flit about to find a coign of vantage. Robert Lowe it was who cynically remarked that he seemed morbidly anxious to throw away his natural advantages! His movements attracted the more notice because he always wore creaking shoes. The point of my story is Disraeli's *mot* about him. After studying him for some time he remarked, "I thought an Irish Member was always either a gentleman or a blackguard, but he's neither!"

And Disraeli's inquiry about another Irish Member may be worth adding here. Joseph Biggar, the Parnellite obstructionist, had marked peculiarities both of figure and gait. When Disraeli first saw him walking up the floor of the House, he looked at him intently through his eyeglass—and, by the way, he always held his eyeglass with his thumb and first finger wrapped round it as if it were an unfamiliar sort of optical instrument—and then, turning to a friend behind him, he asked, "What is that?"

Before I dismiss the subject of "Gosset's room," I may mention that an indiscretion committed there one night very nearly brought it to an untimely end. In Gosset's absence a number of the habitués held an impromptu concert; and owing to some one's "telling tales out of school," Grenville Murray got hold of the story, and a thinly veiled notice of it appeared in *The Queen's Messenger*, a short-lived racy paper of that period. The report gave what purported to be the programme, which, I remember, included a song by the late Duke of Devonshire, who was referred to as "that ungainly youth, Lord Larkington." The Speaker, Mr. Denison, was then getting old and crusty, and he was furious. But Captain Gosset's unbounded popularity in the House saved the situation, and the crisis was averted.

To that popularity it was that he afterwards owed his promotion. Lord Charles Russell, the then Sergeant-at-Arms, had been appointed by the Prime Minister, and when he resigned in 1875 it was assumed that the office was in Mr. Disraeli's gift, and that, as a matter of course, the Assistant Sergeant-at-Arms would succeed to it.

It transpired, however, that in sanctioning Lord Charles's appointment, the Queen had directed that future vacancies were to be reported to the Sovereign, with whom personally the patronage rested. And it was rumoured that Her Majesty intended to confer the office upon the gentleman who at present holds it. But so strong was the feeling of the House on the subject that Disraeli went to Osborne to lay the matter before the Queen. On the day of his return I went down to the Lobby to seek for news. But the Lobby was empty, and I was driven to apply to the principal doorkeeper. The subordinate officials of the House have sometimes to act as "chuckers-out," but never before, perhaps, did a door-keeper act as "chucker-in." Indeed, his passing a stranger into the House, save by express orders, might in ordinary circumstances have cost him his place. But the moment he recognised me, he seized hold of me and rushed me in under the gallery; and I was just in time to see the Premier rise to answer a question on the subject.

He began by stating, with great solemnity and in his grandest manner, that "the appointment of Sergeant-at-Arms was in the gift and entirely in the gift of H.M. the Queen, and there is no person, whatever his position in the House, who has any influence whatever in that appointment." Here he paused, and his words were received in lugubrious silence, as indicating seemingly the failure of his visit to Osborne. Then he added, "But I have been commanded by the Queen to state that, being aware of the strong, not to say unanimous, feeling of the House on the subject, H.M. as a gracious favour to Her faithful Commons has been pleased to appoint to the office the gentleman who is at present Assistant Sergeant-at-Arms." The tumultuous cheering which followed from every corner of a crowded House was a striking testimony to Gosset's popularity.

My relations with him and Lord Charles Russell made me punctilious in all my dealings with their subordinates. With them I played no tricks. But the House of Lords officials were fair game. On the last evening of the great historic debate on the Irish Church, an old friend of my father's, whom I met at dinner, spoke of his fruitless efforts to get an order for the Peers' Gallery, and declared that he would give £100 for a seat. When we rose from dinner I asked him to accompany me to Westminster. I passed with him through the lobbies and up to the gallery door, and there, with the lordliest manner I could assume, I told the doorkeeper that I should be extremely obliged if he could find a seat for my friend. Whom he took me for I never knew, but he responded effusively, and begged me to bring him in. Later on I noticed that he and a colleague were evidently discussing me, trying no doubt to make out who I was. So I thought it better to "skip," as the Yankees say; but my friend kept his seat till the House rose. In passing out I thanked the doorkeeper in a patronising tone for his courtesy, and expressed my regret that I could not stay longer myself. I should add, perhaps, that I never got that £100! But this is a prolonged digression.

Most people will be surprised to hear that according to the Act of Union and the theory of the Constitution, Ireland is under the Home Office, and that the Home Secretary is the Minister responsible to Parliament for Irish affairs. What then, it will be asked, is the position of the Chief Secretary for Ireland? The answer is that, strictly speaking, there is no such office. The Minister who is thus popularly designated is "Chief Secretary to the Lord-Lieutenant," and all official communications are supposed to pass between the Lord-Lieutenant and the Secretary of State. In theory the "Irish Office" is merely a branch of the Chief Secretary's Office at Dublin Castle—a *pied-à-terre* for the Irish officials while in London. All this is now practically changed; but the theory remains, and the change has taken place within recent years. At the time of which I am speaking all important papers relating to Ireland were transmitted to the Home Office, the prescribed form of letter being "I am directed by the Lord-Lieutenant to transmit to you," &c., &c. The proposed scheme was that, instead of this cumbersome system, official papers should be "minuted" to me, and that I should, as it were, represent the Irish Office at Whitehall, and Whitehall at the Irish Office. Mr. Hardy suggested that I should be called "Assistant Secretary for Irish Business," but to this Lord Mayo objected as trenching on his preserves.

Unless a man be so degraded as to like office work for its own sake, the charm of life in a Government Department largely depends on the *personnel*. Practice at the Bar brings one into contact with many people whom one would not choose as companions for a wet day in a villa house. And I have known men even in high positions to whom a like remark would apply. But with such chiefs as Mr. Hardy, Mr. Liddell, and Sir James Ferguson at the Home Office, and Lord Mayo and Sir Thomas Larcom at Dublin Castle, my position was an enviable one. And with the Home Office staff my relations were friendly and pleasant.

The Chief Clerk, indeed, resented my presence, but his influence was a negligible quantity. He was a man of private fortune, who used the Home Office as a pastime. With exemplary regularity he took his two months' annual leave every autumn, and he did comparatively little during the other ten. This, indeed, was quite characteristic of the Home Office in those days. One of the senior clerks, with whom I struck up a friendship, remonstrated with me for my activity and zeal. On his first joining the Department, as he told me, the then Chief Clerk impressed on him that the way to get on in the Civil Service was to do as little as possible, and to do it as quietly as possible. And he himself prospered by acting on that excellent advice. For in due course he rose to the top; and I may add that his tenure of the Chief Clerkship made it clear that the office was unnecessary, and it was abolished when he retired on a pension,

Forty years ago work in the Home Office was light, and it was left to an industrious minority of the staff. Not a few of the clerks were habitual idlers. The office hours were from 11 to 5. It was a nominal 11 and a punctual 5; and much of the intervening time was devoted to luncheon, gossip, and the newspapers. Matters of public interest also claimed attention, such as, for instance, the future of public men who happened to be then coming into notice. Whether Sir George Trevelyan or Sir Charles Dilke was destined to be the future leader of the Liberal party, was a frequent subject of discussion. And as a relief from such grave questions, bets were made as to whether more vehicles would pass up the street or down the street within a specified time, or as to the colour of the horses.

The room assigned to me at first was a Private Secretary's room, adjoining that of the Secretary of State, upon the main floor. But after the change of Government, Lord Macduff (now the Duke of Fife) came in as Assistant Private Secretary, and Mr. Bruce asked me to make way for him. It was while thus temporarily occupying a room upstairs among the clerks that I became free of what might be called the club life of the Office. What I then heard of past escapades prepared me for experiences that followed. One of these many stories recurs to me. One day, in Sir George Grey's time, a battle royal was raging in the Registry, and a tape-tied bundle of official papers, aimed at the head of a "pal," went through the window, and barely missed bonneting the Secretary of State as he passed out on his way to the House of Commons. This occurred at 12 o'clock on a Wednesday, and the delinquent —Nubbles was our pet name for him—forthwith took refuge in one of the smallest apartments in the building, and there he hid himself, a prey to the gloomiest forebodings, until six hours afterwards he was induced to open the door, on hearing that "the House was up," and that the Chief had gone home.

One of the older men, whose room was opposite mine, spent half his time in dodging his duns. He was in a chronic state of impecuniosity; and toward the end of the month, when the pay-dockets were due, he had such a succession of visitors that official work was impossible. At times, indeed, he had to keep in hiding. This was easy in that rabbit-warren of a building, especially as he had an ally in the messenger on our floor, an old man of pompous manners, who had been butler in the house of a previous Secretary of State. The style in which this man played with the unfortunate creditors was a comedy worthy of the stage. Shortly afterwards our friend was discharged with a pension. He commuted his pension for a lump sum, and immediately bolted to America, without venturing to pay even a flying visit to the Office. A search of his room brought to light a number of draft wills, written of course on official paper, by which he made liberal provision for his special chums on the staff!

The ways of the place reminded me of my school days. On my arrival one morning I found a note from Sir James Ferguson's private secretary—his intimates called him "Creeper"—announcing that at three o'clock precisely an old hat, lately the property of the Chief Clerk, would be kicked off from the end of the corridor, and requesting the favour of my presence. When Big Ben struck three I heard "Creeper's" cheery voice ring out, "All on side: Play!" We all turned out, and the game began. On emerging from an unusually hot "scrimmage," I became conscious of the presence of a stranger at my side, a timid little Frenchman, who meekly inquired, "Is dis de office for de naturalisation?" It was!

There were escapades also of another kind. During a smallpox epidemic at this time, a supply of lymph reached the Home Office; for in those days the Home Office dealt with all matters of that kind. One of the clerks—he afterwards succeeded to a Peerage—at once "requisitioned" for a new eraser, and proceeded to vaccinate himself and all whom he could induce to be operated on. The after-condition of his victims

—I was not of the number—gave proof that the lymph was good!

"Making hay" in a man's room was one of the stock amusements. On coming back from luncheon one day I found every movable article of every kind which my room contained piled up on my table, and Lord Granville's private secretary—Mr. (afterwards Sir Robert) Meade—standing in the middle of the floor surveying the pyramid. He had called on some important Foreign Office business. This was too much for me. I told no tales, but I represented to the Chief that I found it very inconvenient to be upstairs, and a room on the main floor was again assigned to me.

My pen might run on indefinitely in this vein, but the foregoing may suffice to indicate what life in the Home Office was like a generation ago. In those days there were no "Lower-division clerks" or "Civil Service writers." And not even the sub-departments were housed under the same roof as the Secretary of State until after we moved into the new edifice in August, 1875. We had the place to ourselves.

Some little historic interest attaches to the old building, on account of its connection with the ancient Palace of Whitehall, on the site of which it stands. The room I first occupied looked out on a small yard which must have been within the Palace, and in that yard was an iron cistern which bore date the year after the great Fire of London. This, by the way, suggests an incursion into constitutional history. The " Whitehall " from which the Home Secretary dates his official letters is not the street of that name, but the Palace. And the title " Principal Secretary of State" does not, as people suppose, distinguish the Minister from his subordinates, but points back to the origin of the office. Originally the Sovereign dealt with affairs of State through his private secretary. But in course of time it became necessary to appoint a special secretary to take charge of such matters; and the Secretary of State was designated H.M.'s " Principal Secretary." As State affairs have increased in volume and importance the duties have been again and again divided, and additional " Principal Secretaries of State " have been appointed to take control of special departments; but while these date their letters from their respective offices, " Whitehall " remains the proper official address of the Home Secretary as the lineal descendant and heir of the original " Principal Secretary of State."

" The New Home Office " to which I have referred is a marvellous triumph of architectural skill. No one but a real genius could have designed a great building which, from it main plan down to its smallest detail, is absolutely unsuited to the purpose for which it was intended. The "grand staircase" ends at a half landing from which an inferior set of stairs leads to the principal floor. And a dark passage on that floor leads to the principal rooms. The Secretary of State's room was originally so ill-lighted that an important structural alteration was needed to make it habitable, and even when so altered, Sir William Harcourt fitly likened it to a railway station waiting-room. So great was his aversion to it, indeed, that he spent most of his official hours in his house in Grafton Street.

The building, as viewed from the street, contains only three floors above the basement. But as in fact there are four, one window has to do duty on two floors. The result is that the second floor rooms are like bear-pits, the windows being placed so high that no one can see the opposite houses from them, much less the street. And in the upper rooms the windows reach but three feet from the floor. But as, in an office, light is wanted above the table and not under it, no one of these rooms could be brought into use until, at considerable cost, a skylight had been inserted in the massive fireproof roof.

The Old Home Office and the New

Burglars trouble us at times, but we suffer from architects every day of our lives. And yet it seems incredible that the innumerable and glaring faults of that building are due to incompetence or accident. The explanation current at Whitehall was that Sir Gilbert Scott deliberately set himself to spite the Government for rejecting his original plans.

In the new building the clerks did not play football surreptitiously in the corridors, but after office hours we played tennis openly in the inner court (now choked by an iron shed). The habitués were Lushington, the Assistant Under-Secretary; Sir J. E. Moss, the Private Secretary; Charles Murdoch (afterwards Assistant Under-Secretary), and myself. Grand games we used to have, the fastest tennis, indeed, that I ever played, and one hour of it was ample exercise for a whole day.

To what extent "upstairs life" in the other Government Offices forty years ago resembled that of the Home Office I cannot aver from personal knowledge. But I can testify that all that has been written about "red tape" and "the circumlocution office" applied to those of them with which I had much to do; though, having regard to the confidential nature of my work, I was specially introduced to the Under-

Secretaries of the various departments, and they always received me with courtesy and kindness.

This was specially notable in the case of the Foreign Office, for the Under-Secretary, Mr. (afterwards Lord) Hammond, was singularly unbending in official life. He was the very impersonation of "red tape." I am reminded of one of my visits to him. He received me promptly and kindly, as he always did, but he scouted my mission. The Irish Government wished me to obtain the Foreign Office verification of the Chief Secretary's signature to an important document, and to telegraph to Dublin when I had procured it. In Lord Mayo's well-known signature the final "o" stood apart, with a sort of curl above it. "I—I—I should have thought it was May 6," said Hammond! My personal testimony went for nothing. The official documents in the case, which I had received from Dublin Castle, he refused even to look at. The fact that Lord Mayo was a Cabinet Minister did not matter. He could not recognise the Irish Government; he knew only the Home Office, and he could not verify the signature unless it came before him duly certified by the Under-Secretary of State for the Home Department. In a word, he kept to the letter of the law, that Ireland was under the Home Office, and to the etiquette of the service, that he would only deal with the Under-Secretary.

At the War Office, on the other hand, the Chiefs were always ready to comply with any demand, but "the Office" was the difficulty. One morning, for example, on receipt of an urgent letter from Dublin Castle asking me to procure the attestation paper of a certain soldier, I repaired to Pall Mall, expecting to obtain it at once. But no one seemed to know where it was to be found; and the letter which brought me the document later in the day had a postscript to the effect that they had not yet discovered which branch of the Office dealt with attestation papers!

My description of life in the Home Office when I first entered it might seem to discredit Mr. Liddell, the Under-Secretary. I wish to guard against that suggestion. It was in his reign that the reorganisation took place which inaugurated the present era of efficiency. But he had then come fresh from practising at the Bar, and he had no knowledge of a Government Office. And in those days there was no Assistant Under-Secretary; and, as already intimated, the Chief Clerk was a cipher, so that he had no one to coach him. He was quite admirable in managing the Office. On the rare occasions when he was ruffled or vexed, his bearing realised the schoolboy's definition of righteous anger: to wit, "being angry without swearing." And if at times he used language that would spoil the sale of a Sunday School book, it betokened in his case a placid serenity of temper. And matters that might disturb the equanimity of a different type of man he disposed of with dignified calm.

I recall an incident which may serve to illustrate what I mean. A teacup storm was raging as to which branch of the Office should be charged with certain work, and a minute of Liddell's, directing the "Domestic Department" to write a certain letter, brought about a crisis. I was with him in his room when the head of that department (Knyvett, afterwards Sir Carey Knyvett) bustled in, and laying the document in question on Liddell's desk, delivered himself of an elaborate protest against the decision. His only response was a long-drawn "Oh," followed by a single word—it was a word that is never heard in the drawing-room—and then he resumed his work. After a while he rose with a beaming face, and picking up the paper, as though for the first time, he handed it back to Knyvett with, "Look here, old chap, will you get that letter written for my signature?" Like "the venerable Jacob" in the ballad, Knyvett "smole a sickly smile," and giving me a helpless sort of look, he cleared out. That teacup storm was at an end. I might give dozens of similar incidents, but this may suffice to show the sort of man the Under-Secretary was. His imperturbable bonhomie succeeded where severity might have set the Office by the ears. But behind his bonhomie there was so much dignity, and such a sense of reserve power, that no one ever presumed upon it.

All the more remarkable this, from the fact that, not infrequently, his ways were those of a jovial schoolboy, rather than of a staid official of aristocratic proclivities. I have been on easy terms with not a few of the men under whom I have served, but none of them unbended as Liddell did. This showed itself at times even in his instructions to me in official work. His "minutes" were always written with care, and they were usually both clear and able. But much of my work was of such a confidential or personal nature that his directions were given to me either *viva voce*, or in private notes. And to this day I can laugh over some of these.

Here is a sample. When the Fenians were smuggling revolvers and rifles into Ireland, labelled as pianos, or butter, or cement, I proposed that the clandestine conveyance of firearms should be made an offence. The Secretary of State adopted my *projet de loi*, and it was referred to the Treasury Counsel (Mr.—afterwards Lord—Thring) to draft the Bill. But, instead of acting on Mr. Bruce's instructions, he wrote back a strong letter of objection and protest. Even the Magistrates, he said, would regard such an enactment as unworkable. This was referred to Bow Street, and the Chief Magistrate replied that he and his colleagues approved of the scheme, and saw no practical difficulty in giving effect to it. Liddell's minute to me on this, written on a sheet of notepaper, was in the following terms: "Thring is getting —— bumptious. Prepare a letter to him for my signature. Just tell him to go to —— and square the circle; you know how to put it." I did!

In a similar vein it was that he received my congratulations the day he was gazetted a K.C.B. Rising from his table he faced me on the hearth-rug, and presently said he, his blank stare giving way to a genial smile, "But isn't it awful rot being called 'Sir'!" As a contemporary philosopher, known to fame as "Josh Billings," has said, "Gravity becomes a fool at all times; a wise man upon state occasions." These were not state occasions, and Liddell was no fool.

CHAPTER IV

The change of Government in 1868—Mr. Henry Bruce as Secretary of State—Revival of Fenian activity—Michael Davitt's life-story—Activity in revolutionary circles in 1870—Informant "Maxwell"—Count d'Orsay's death—"The Waterloo Bridge mystery" of 1857—Life in lodgings: with Charles Reade and Mrs. Seymour—Reade's literary work—A buttered egg supper—J. A. Froude and his view of the Irish Question.

As I review the earlier years of my life in London, I wish to keep silence about all matters of a specially confidential nature, and at the same time to avoid loading these pages with mere gossip and trivial details. I am the only survivor of those who had knowledge of the graver matters to which I allude; and while the disclosure of them now would lend sensational interest to my story, it would serve no useful public purpose. Apart from these, indeed, incidents abounded which might, with a little dressing up, afford material for a novel. I was in a position, moreover, to know all that was worth knowing in the sphere of ordinary Police work at Scotland Yard. For Sir Richard Mayne had placed the detective department at my disposal; and as I soon gained the confidence and good-will of the officers, they not only helped me loyally in my inquiries respecting political crime, but spoke to me without reserve about their "cases" and all ordinary Police business. All this, however, is ancient history, and the years in question shall be dismissed with no more notice than is necessary to preserve the sequence of my narrative.

At that time I had no intention of abandoning the profession of my choice, and it was not till ten years later that I entered the Civil Service. My immediate objective was admission to the English Bar. For though a sceptic both by temperament and training, I have long held a firm belief in the capacity of Irish agitators to impose upon English statesmen—a belief that is shared by all Irishmen, not excepting the agitators themselves—and, as I anticipated the evils which agitation has in fact brought upon Ireland, I wished to be free of the Law Courts at Westminster as well as in Dublin.

I may here say once for all that, though called to the English Bar, I never engaged in Court practice in England. For every time I tried to break free from Government work something occurred to make me postpone the crisis. Mr. Liddell's friendship had much to do with it. He had a magnetic influence over me; and he always urged me to remain at Whitehall, assuring me again and again that I was "certain to get something good." When the change of Government occurred in December, 1868, I seriously contemplated going back to Ireland. Not on the score of party politics—for I have never been a party man—but because, as I have already said, my friendly relations with my official chiefs weighed much with me, and on that account I feared a change of masters. "I don't know how you feel, but I'm devilish miserable," was Liddell's greeting to me the day the change took place. But it is not the wicked only who are disquieted in vain. For the change of masters served only to bring me new friends. And as regards the political element involved, I cannot but contrast the change of December, 1868, with that of December, 1905; for Mr. Bruce at once announced that he was satisfied that everything approved by Mr. Hardy must be right, and all was to go on as usual in the Office.

Not that he was a weak man. He was in fact one of the best Home Secretaries of my time—

a man of judgment and discretion, a thorough gentleman, a good lawyer, and a pleasing speaker. But on the staff of two of the leading newspapers there were certain Government officials who, for some reason or other, were his enemies. One of them was a Metropolitan Police magistrate, and the other was still more closely connected with Scotland Yard; and the persistent efforts of these journalists conveyed to the public a wholly false impression of Mr. Bruce's adminstration of the Home Office. He was prejudiced also by appointing as his Private Secretary a man who, though clever and amiable, was wanting in tact and common sense.

The absurd Fenian scare which followed "the Clerkenwell explosion" naturally led to a revival of Fenian activity. Ricard Burke, who instigated that outrage, was succeeded by Michael Davitt as "arms agent" to the conspirators, and, unlike most of their paid officials, he served them honestly and well. So much so, indeed, that during the year 1869 the illicit introduction of arms into Ireland became a matter of anxiety to the Irish Government. And such is the fatuity of Government methods and ways, that this very time was chosen by the War Office to sell off stores of discarded rifles. The Fenians were thus enabled to purchase at "knock-out" prices better arms than had ever been carried by British troops in actual warfare; and quantities of these were smuggled into Ireland for the use of the rebels. We were aware of what was doing; but there is a great difference between getting information and obtaining evidence for a treason-felony prosecution, and it was not till February, 1870, that Davitt and his partner in the business fell into our clutches.

Davitt's life-story is not without interest. When he was but twelve years of age an accident in a Lancashire cotton mill cost him the loss of one of his arms. Being thus unfitted for manual labour, he hawked newspapers for a stationer in a small Lancashire town. And it was while thus engaged that he was drawn into the meshes of Fenianism. At the time of his conviction, therefore, he was personally of no account whatever. But his good conduct as a prisoner, and his evident desire to use any opportunities allowed him of self-improvement, attracted the notice of Mr. William Fagan, the Visiting Director, who encouraged and helped him in many ways. His influence with the convict was all the greater because he was a fellow-countryman of his and a co-religionist. And as the result the Davitt of the Land League was a very different man from the ignorant fellow who was sent to penal servitude in 1870. As so many hard things are said about the discipline of convict prisons, it deserves to be recorded that it was in a convict prison that Davitt acquired his fitness for the part he afterwards played as Parnell's ally in the Irish land war, and he freely acknowledged this upon occasions.

The year 1870 was marked by a good deal of activity in revolutionary circles. And the break up of the French Secret Service Department, on the fall of the Empire, brought me much useful and interesting information. For several of the secret agents of the *Sureté* came to London, and some of them applied to me for employment. Among them was one of the most remarkable men I have ever met in this sort of work. Maxwell was the *nom de guerre* I gave him. His physique, and notably his head, might have gained him a living as an artist's model. He spoke many languages, and his experiences as a revolutionist, and afterwards as a Police agent, would have made a thrilling story.

Some of the matters he disclosed to me have an historic interest. Count d'Orsay was supposed to have died of spine-disease and a carbuncle in the back. As a matter of fact the carbuncle was a euphemism for a bullet aimed at the Emperor as they were walking together in the gardens of the Elysée. The facts were carefully suppressed, but Maxwell was in the secret. I received confirmation of this afterwards from the *Chef de la Sureté* in Paris. The matter had a peculiar interest for me, as my father was Lady Harriet d'Orsay's lawyer, and the Count valued his friendship. Among his gifts to him, now in my possession, was a tortoise-shell and gold snuff-box bearing an exquisite miniature of Louis XVI.

Another of Maxwell's disclosures will be of interest to thousands of Londoners who have passed middle age. Of all the London horrors of our time, none ever made a greater sensation than the "Waterloo Bridge Mystery" of 1857. On one of the buttresses of the bridge a carpet-bag was found on the morning of the 9th of October of that year, containing certain mutilated fragments of a human body. The evidence given at the inquest made it clear that a foul and brutal murder had been committed, but no clue could be discovered to the identity of either the victim or the assassins. Maxwell gave me the facts in full detail. And inquiries made through the Foreign Office and Scotland Yard brought confirmation of all the main points of his story.

The victim was an Italian Police agent who

had been sent to London on a special mission. Posing as a revolutionist, he put up at a house in Cranbourne Street, Soho, frequented by Italians of that class. Revolutionists are proverbially suspicious of one another, and a glaring indiscretion cost the man his life. He not only preserved a letter of instructions about his work, but carried it in his pocket; and this letter his companions got hold of by searching his clothes when he was asleep. As he mounted the stairs the next night in company with some of his fellow-lodgers, he received a blow on the head that stunned him, and his body was dragged to the basement. There he recovered consciousness, but a brief struggle was quickly ended by the use of the assassins' knives. They proceeded to cut up the body, and several nights were spent in efforts to get rid of the remains by burning them. This, however, proved a tedious and irksome task, and it was decided to jettison the rest of the corpse in the river.

One of Maxwell's last visits to me was marked by a dramatic incident which illustrates what secret service work at times involves. The time had come when I could no longer make use of him, and I wrote to tell him so. He called by appointment at my private house, and seated in my dining-room he deliberately announced his intention of committing suicide. For if only he were out of the way, he said, he could rely on friends to help his wife and daughter. At the same time he asked me to accept some valuable papers in return for my kindness to him. "You are going to kill yourself, leaving your wife and daughter to charity in a strange land?" I asked. He assented with imperturbable calmness. "Then," said I, "I'll write you down a coward and a scoundrel." He sprang at me like a wounded tiger. His fingers twitched convulsively, and he seemed about to grip me by the throat. I was standing on the hearthrug with my hands behind my back, and, without moving a muscle, I looked him steadily in the face. Presently all the passion died out of him, and falling back into his seat he utterly broke down. I left the room for some ten minutes, and on my return I handed him the papers he had brought me; and when he came back to me a week later, I found that, as I hoped, he had abandoned all thought of self-destruction.

I have alluded to my making the acquaintance of literary men of note at this time. The circumstances in which I came to know one of the number are so characteristic of the man that I am tempted to record them. Life in London lodgings is not usually deemed ideal, but my experiences in that regard were pleasant. And after living for a brief interval in the Westminster Palace Hotel as a member of the "Crown Club" —the acorn from which grew the oak of the "St. Stephen's," now palatially housed opposite the clock tower at Westminster—I decided to return to lodgings. Accordingly I engaged rooms in Park Lane in a house rented by a house-agent who used the ground-floor as his office. But the day before I was to take possession he called on me at Whitehall and appealed to me to waive my right to the rooms, as his former tenant had changed plans and wished to remain with him. That very afternoon, he added, he had been commissioned to let some exceptionally nice apartments at Albert Gate, overlooking Hyde Park: would I consent to look at them? I consented, and at once went off to view the house he indicated.

I was received by a charming matronly lady, and the rooms shown me were as charming as herself. Paintings worth thousands of pounds adorned the walls, including Sir Joshua Reynolds's portrait of the Chevalier d'Éon. I suggested that they would probably expect a higher rent than I was prepared to pay. How much was I prepared to pay? she asked.

I named the amount asked for at Park Lane, and without another word the matter was settled. I was amazed that folk so wealthy should let lodgings, and that, too, without even requiring a reference from me. But I had no fears of my portmanteaux being seized by bailiffs in a house that held such art treasures, and I moved in next day. Not till then did I discover that the house was Charles Reade's, and that my charming landlady was Mrs. Seymour.

No one who knew the great novelist, or who has read his "Life," needs to be told who Mrs. Seymour was. With ringing laughter she afterwards gave me the whole story. Reade had received a letter from some relatives for whom he had no love, to say they were coming to town to sponge on him. He fumed and stormed. "Put the rooms on a house-agent's books," he exclaimed, "and write and tell them you have done so, and that they mustn't come." Having thus delivered his soul, he went off to Oxford, where his fellowship at Magdalen afforded him a pleasant retreat. Two hours afterwards Mrs. Seymour had carried out his wishes, I called and engaged the rooms. Finding me there on his return to town set him fuming even worse than before. He wouldn't have lodgers in his house, he declared, and I must be turned out at once. But Mrs. Seymour knew how to manage him, and I was left in possession. For a time, however, he ignored me. The first advance he ever made was his writing me the following note, on hearing that the dog had disturbed me in the night:—

"I am truly concerned to hear that the wild beast which governs and oppresses this house kept you awake with his howling last night; I heard him, but owing to the echoes of this spacious mansion, could not divine where our tormentor was.

"Should this recur, please entice him into your room and leather him. This has always a soothing influence on him. But indeed I shall endeavour to restrain his wanderings in future, at all events during the small hours."

This was a "Dear Sir"; but before long we struck up a friendship, and I received many kindnesses from him. So much so, indeed, that he used to lend me his own pet room when I invited men to dinner, and sometimes he joined my party. It was the room he had built in his garden abutting on Hyde Park. In that same room, by the way, looking out on "the trees of the nation," as he phrased it, is laid one of the chief scenes in "A Terrible Temptation."

Reade's literary work was a rare combination

of genius and plodding. A brass scuttle which stood by the fireplace held the illustrated and other papers which reached him week by week. From these he culled anything that took his fancy, and the cuttings were thrown into a companion scuttle, to be afterwards inserted in scrap-books, and duly indexed. Materials for his novels and plays were thus supplied or suggested. The accuracy of his descriptions of events and places was phenomenal. Frederick Locker once told me that he read "Never too Late to Mend" while at the gold-diggings in Australia, and as again and again he looked up from the book to view the scene so graphically portrayed in its pages, the vividness and accuracy of the description amazed and delighted him. Had Reade ever visited Australia? No bribe, I told him, could tempt the great novelist to cross the ocean. I was once asked to put before him a very flattering proposal for a lecture tour in America. I gave him the particulars, ending by naming the proffered fee of I forget how many thousand pounds. "Tell them to make it millions," was the only answer he vouchsafed to it!

Though I couldn't write "Never too Late to Mend," I could make "buttered eggs"; and as Reade watched the operation in my room one night, his looks and words suggested that he thought the cooking more wonderful than the writing. We had met at the hall door on his return home very hungry from a theatrical supper, at which, as he explained, there was a division of labour, he doing the talking and the others the eating. In his handkerchief he had some baked potatoes, purchased at a stall which stood nightly in the street opposite his house; and his apology for not offering to share them with me was that in his room he had neither knife, fork, nor plate. So I begged him to come upstairs with me, and I disclosed to him the contents of my cupboard, which included all that was needed for an impromptu supper, not excepting a loaf and butter, eggs, a saucepan, and an Etna. As already intimated, the process of making scrambled eggs excited his admiration, and from that hour I believe he regarded his lodger as a personage.

It was in Ireland that at this time I made the acquaintance of Mr. Froude, the historian. For some years he rented Lord Lansdowne's charming summer cottage on the Kenmare River; and while living at Dereen he struck up a friendship with special friends of mine, whose beautiful homes on the Kerry side of the estuary I used to visit during my summer trips to Ireland. The acquaintance thus formed led to my becoming a contributor to *Frazer*. Among my papers I find the following letter from Mr. Froude, and I reproduce it here because it is as applicable to the misgovernment of Ireland to-day as when it was written a generation ago. It refers to an Irish article of mine to which he gave the place of honour in one number of the magazine :—

"I entirely agree with you about the Government policy, which is in fact abdicating command, and leaving the mutinous part of the crew to manage the vessel. At present the only good which can be done is to enforce the law rigidly, and to place in all situations of trust and confidence in the country those who are loyal to the connection between England and Ireland (Catholic or Protestant), and no others. Unfortunately the surest road to favour has been disloyalty."

CHAPTER V

The Royal Commission on Railway Accidents—Treasury ways—The Royal Observatory of Edinburgh Commission—Mr. Chamberlain's Commission on Loss of Life at Sea—The importance of a good luncheon—H.R.H. the Duke of Edinburgh's friendship—Appointed to the Prison Commission and became a Civil servant—Relations with the chairman, Sir E. F. du Cane—The *personnel* of the Commission—Admiral Wyndham Hornby and a Stock Exchange story—A tribute to Sir E. du Cane—Prison Reforms: the "humanitarians" and the Prevention of Crimes Bill—More about Treasury meanness—A Secret Service Fund salary in violation of the statute—Application to Sir H. Ibbetson as to pension.

As already intimated, it was in 1877 that, on the passing of the Prison Act of that year, I entered the Civil Service. The preceding years were spent both pleasantly and profitably. As the Treasury ignored my existence, I held myself ree from all the disabilities and restrictions of a Civil Service appointment. I had a fair amount of leisure, of course, and my purse profited by the use of my pen. I also served on various Government Commissions. Of the Royal Commission on Railway Accidents I have the pleasantest memories, for it was in connection with it that I made one of the most valued friendships of this period of my life. The Commission was appointed in 1874 under the chairmanship of the then Duke of Buckingham. There were irreconcilable interests represented on it, and the Chairman proved quite incapable of bringing matters to an issue. It seemed likely to end in a fiasco; and when the Duke received an Indian appointment, the Secretary of State appealed to the Earl of Aberdeen to accept the chairmanship and try to bring the labours of the Commission to a practical and useful end.

The Home Secretary asked me to take the secretaryship, and to give my best help to the new Chairman. This was early in 1876; but some valuable time was lost owing to the characteristic action of the Treasury. It appeared that the Duke had taken my predecessor abroad with him, intending to draft the report of the Commission during his voyage to India. And when I took over the work I found the accounts in such a hopeless muddle that I could not venture to accept any responsibility for them. Lord Aberdeen accordingly called a meeting of the Commission and explained matters to his colleagues; and as the result I was directed to write to the Treasury, detailing all the circumstances, and asking for money to enable us to carry out the wishes of the Secretary of State. In due course my letter brought me a reply which was unusually offensive even for the Treasury. I put it aside and took no notice of it. Happening to meet one of my Treasury friends in the Park one morning on my way to Whitehall, we walked down together. He asked me what I was doing on the Commission. I told him I was drawing my salary with scrupulous care, but that the Commissioners had decided not to hold another meeting until I had received an "imprest" from the Treasury. That very afternoon he called on me—it was the late Sir William Brampton Gurdon—and asked me to let him take back the offensive epistle. The following week I received a letter in which, without any reference to their former effusion, "my Lords" sent me the imprest I had asked for.

When at last we met for business it looked as if the Commission would end in a wrangle; but Lord Aberdeen's imperturbable bonhomie at last prevailed. The Duke's draft report, which had been circulated to the members, was scouted; and a series of resolutions, adopted after discussion, became the basis of a report which the new Chairman undertook to prepare during the autumn recess. The Commission met again on the 14th of November (1876); and on the 2nd of February following, this new report was signed.

The Royal Observatory of Edinburgh Commission, on which also I was engaged during 1876, deserves a passing notice. Every task of the kind won for me new friends, and in this connection I gained the friendship of the Royal Astronomer and Mrs. Piazzi Smythe. I should mention also the Chairman, Lord Lindsay (now Earl of Crawford), and Professor Tait; and the acquaintance I then formed with Sir George Airy, the Astronomer-Royal, proved valuable to me afterwards in some of my literary work. One of the chief points in the inquiry was the failure of the transit instrument of the Observatory. The instrument was mounted on two stone pillars, each a monolith, let down into the rock of the Calton Hill. It was seemingly "one of the most stable things on earth with which to measure the movements of the stars." Thus it was that Professor Piazzi Smythe described it. But he went on to explain that, owing to the extrordinary nature of the stone of the piers, the heat of the little lantern which an astronomer uses in his work sufficed to warp them to such an extent as to throw the instrument out of gear. And much of the work of the Observatory had been thus rendered valueless during all the years before the mystery of the stone had been discovered.

I had remonstrated against my being appointed on such a Commission, for, as I told the Secretary of State, I did not know the difference between a transit instrument and a pump; but I became so interested in the inquiry that at its close I was able to write the report which led to the removal of the Observatory from the Calton Hill to its present site.

This duty devolved on me unexpectedly. The Chairman of the Commission had announced his intention of preparing the report himself. But during my summer holiday I had a letter from him to say he was medically ordered to avoid all work for a while, and he asked me to relieve him of the task. He was good enough to express cordial appreciation of my draft, and accepted it without any material alteration. I had no difficulty in getting the signatures of all the Commissioners except the Astronomer-Royal, who, Lord Lindsay declared, would sign the report only out of compliment to himself; and as it was not his own drafting, that consideration lapsed. And yet he felt that the absence of Sir George

Airy's signature would greatly impair its value. It was not that as an astronomer he would hesitate to endorse the proposals of the report. But he and Piazzi Smythe never could "hit it off," for as men they were as unlike as men could be. Airy therefore would have found more satisfaction in thwarting his Scottish colleague than in helping him. But I was conceited enough to promise that I would obtain his signature. So I made for Greenwich and laid the document before him. After he had read it, I talked so incessantly that I gave him no chance to ask me any questions which would have compelled me to declare myself the writer of it. Then, rising hurriedly, I said I had promised Lord Lindsay to return by such a train; would he kindly let me go? He took up his pen and added his signature!

In this connection I will notice also the Royal Commission on Loss of Life at Sea, although it belongs to a later date (1884), when Sir William Harcourt was Secretary of State. That Commission was the outcome of a controversy raised by a statement of Mr. Chamberlain's, as President of the Board of Trade, that the annual loss of life among the sailors on British ships amounted to one in sixty, a statement which, though based on the statistics of his Department, was vehemently scouted by shipowners. Lord Aberdeen's success on the Railway Accidents Commission led to his being asked to preside over this new Commission; and among the most prominent of its members were the Duke of Edinburgh, Mr. Chamberlain himself, and Mr. Justice Butt. Lord Aberdeen was good enough to wish for my help again, and I wrote to Sir William Harcourt, who was then away in the country, asking for the Secretaryship of the Commission. Sir William had recently done me a great injustice, and so, *more suo*, he replied in the kindest terms, assuring me that he would gladly comply if Sir Edmund du Cane had no objection (I was then attached to the Prison Department). Sir Edmund gave his consent most cordially, and in November, 1884, the Commission was appointed with my name as Secretary. On the change of Government in 1886, Lord Aberdeen became Lord-Lieutenant of Ireland, and a new warrant was issued appointing Mr. Shaw Lefevre Chairman, and adding Admiral Sir Cooper Key and Mr. (now Lord) Heneage to the Commission. The report was presented in August, 1887.

In these pages I am dealing only with the lighter side of things, and I have no intention of discussing the merits of Royal Commissions in general, or of this one in particular. But I claim special credit for the result attained in this case. The interests represented seemed irreconcilable, and yet the discussions were amicable, and the report was signed by all the Commissioners. For the public benefit I must reveal the secret of my success. That "an army marches on its stomach" was one of Napoleon's favourite aphorisms. And "feed the brute" was the advice the young wife received from her matronly friend, when she complained of her husband's temper. Here then is my secret. The refreshment allowance sanctioned by the Treasury was so inadequate that "sandwiches and sherry" was the stock luncheon of Royal Commissions; and on the Railway Accidents Commission I often noticed that the members were more intractable after that repast than during the morning sitting. I proposed therefore that we should supplement the Treasury pittance by a general "whip," and have a good "sit down" repast in the Secretary's room. This was agreed to, and I made the necessary arrangements with one of the best West End caterers. The results were marked and manifest. It is not merely that having a comfortable meal and a good cigar soothes the nerves and smooths the temper, but the forty minutes' chat round the luncheon-table brought the Commissioners together socially, and this influenced their discussions in the board-room.

To me personally this was both a pleasure and a benefit on other grounds, for I thus came to make the acquaintance of the members. I may mention specially that I thus gained the honour of the Duke of Edinburgh's friendship. For H.R.H. did not approve of hurrying over the cigar stage of the luncheon recess; and when his colleagues rose, he usually kept me with him. On H.R.H.'s leaving to take up his command in the Mediterranean, he desired me to write to him regularly about the work; and on his return to England he did me the honour of giving many proofs that he had not forgotten me.

Unlike these temporary Commissions, the Prison Commission is a branch of the permanent Civil Service. It is a sub-department of the Home Office, and it was owing to the nature of its initial duties that it had to be constituted as a Commission. The various counties and municipalities of England were formerly responsible to provide accommodation for their prisoners. The Prison Act, 1865, maintained that responsibility, while introducing many reforms, and providing that the prisons should be open to full Government inspection by officers appointed by the Secretary of State. By the Prison Act, 1877, on the other hand, all prisons became vested in the Secretary of State, and all the responsibilities and duties of prison administration were transferred to Government, subject to inspection by committees of justices representing the former Prison Authorities. This change involved elaborate inquiries and accurate records as to the jail accommodation provided in each locality, and as to the services and emoluments of the staff. The extent of these inquiries may be estimated when I add that the prisons thus taken over by Government numbered 112, and that under Government administration this number was reduced to 60.[1]

Mr. (now Viscount) Cross, from whom I had received many favours, asked me to undertake these duties, as Secretary to the Commission. This preliminary task completed, I threw myself *con amore* into the general work of the Department. The Chairman, Sir Edmund du Cane, I had known for years as Chairman of the Directors of Convict Prisons. And though the other Commissioners, and the Inspectors appointed under the statute, were strangers to me, we soon became close friends, and I eagerly responded to their efforts to draw me into their work and to

[1] Convict prisons, being already Government establishments, were not within the Prison Act, 1877.

interest me in all branches of prison administration. But I was now a "Civil Servant," and I came to appreciate the wisdom of the maxim quoted in a previous chapter, "In the Civil Service, do as little as you can, and as quietly as you can." The one man whose goodwill was of practical importance to me was the Chairman, and the more active and zealous I became in the work of the Department, the more unpleasant did my relations become with Sir Edmund du Cane. Indeed, after Sir William Harcourt came to the Home Office his bearing toward me became extremely unpleasant.

One of his special friends at last explained the mystery to me. Du Cane resented there being any communication with the Home Office on Prison matters save by himself, and, as I was in and out of the Under-Secretary's room every day —for Mr. Liddell's friendship for me never flagged—and in my Secret Service work I was frequently closeted with the Secretary of State, Du Cane was jealous of me. I changed front at once. I never visited another prison, nor did I ever do a real day's work again in prison business. When the proofs of my repentance became manifest, I received a dinner invitation from Sir Edmund. Then came week-end invitations to his house at Coombe, and we had many a country walk together, in which we talked on every imaginable subject except prisons. He was my firm friend ever afterwards, and helped me in many ways. The moral of all this may seem very immoral; but, while I vouch for the facts, I disclaim responsibility for the use people may make of them.

Once I had made my peace with the Chairman, we were a pleasant coterie on the Commission. The Commissioners were four in number—Colonel Sir E. F. du Cane, Admiral Wyndham Hornby, afterwards gazetted a K.C.B., Mr. Perry-Watlington, who represented the county Justice element, and Captain Walter Stopford, one of the "Gentlemen Ushers" in the Royal Household. His fitness for the Prison Department was that he had experience of the inside of a prison. An equivocal expression this; but his experience was not acquired as a convict, but as a Prison Governor. He was not only a most valuable member of the Board, but a charming colleague and companion. As Perry-Watlington lived in the country, and came to the Office only as and when the work required his presence, he was kind enough to change rooms with me; and I thus obtained one of the pleasantest rooms in the whole building.

"The Admiral," as we all called him, had the

adjoining room, and he always liked to keep the door between us open. Though he was so much my senior in years, we became regular chums, and he was excellent company. He had many a yarn about his sea-service, and stories innumerable about Knowsley, where he had been "Controller" for twenty years in the days of the great Lord Derby. His Knowsley life brought him into touch with all the great Conservative leaders, and he was well posted in the political gossip of the party. And even if he had been a Civil Servant from his youth up he could not have been fonder of a chat during office hours, especially when he had anything he deemed peculiarly confidential to impart.

This reminds me of an amusing incident which may be worth recounting. "Anderson, I have something to tell you in strict confidence," he announced one morning, as he sat down in my arm-chair. And he went on to tell me, as a State secret, that the Government had a scheme on foot which was certain to benefit Turkey. He had therefore telegraphed that morning to his broker to buy some Turkish Bonds. He then went out, as I afterwards discovered, to give the same tip "in strict confidence" to a number of his special friends in the various Government offices. I was younger than I am now, and the bait took.

Turkish Bonds were quoted that morning at £8, so I decided to go in for a "deal," and I telegraphed to a stockbroker friend to buy for me. The Bonds began to go up, and one day the following week I went into the City to make inquiries about them. Failing to find the broker who had bought for me, I applied to another Stock Exchange acquaintance. He told me that in the City they could learn nothing to explain the rise, but it was evident that something was known in official circles, as one day lately a number of orders to buy had been telegraphed from the different Government offices. I cleared out at £12, and the Bonds soon fell back to their normal value.

I do not know whether this story is typical of Stock Exchange ways, but it is thoroughly typical of Whitehall, and especially of my friend "the Admiral."

I cannot close this chapter without paying my sincere tribute to the great ability of Sir Edmund du Cane, the Chairman of the Commission. Indeed, if only he had been a man of wider sympathies, and his care for prisoners had equalled his knowledge of prisons, he would have been a perfect prison administrator.

Under his rule very great improvements were effected in prisons and prison administration;

and if criminals were mere animals, nothing more need be desired in either sphere. But criminals are human beings, and they ought to be treated as such. Though I say this, I have no sympathy with the professional humanitarians. Their pestilent agitation on behalf of scoundrels who deserve the gallows so offends and irritates all thoughtful and sensible people, that it is not easy to get a hearing for urgently needed reforms in the interests of the mass of the prison population. Their campaign of calumny against me personally, I can treat with contempt, but I deplore and resent their action in hindering reforms with which my name is associated—reforms which would put an end to professional crime, and would change a prison into a reformatory in the case of the weak and the unfortunate.

Thanks to the enlightened administration of our present Prison Board, a great advance has been affected in this direction on behalf of the young. But public opinion will not justify kindred reforms in the interests of adult prisoners until the wicked are separated from the weak. Mr. Gladstone's Prevention of Crimes Bill would have brought such reforms within the sphere of practical politics ; but as the result of an agitation promoted by the professional humanitarians the Bill was turned into a measure for the relief of the professional criminals, who are their special *protégés*.

I will only repeat what I have often said before about prison cells. It is not that they are not large enough. They are larger and better ventilated than the "studies" provided for our boys in the older buildings of some public schools. But what distinguishes a prison cell from every other sort of apartment designed for human habitation is that all view of external nature, such as might soothe and possibly elevate the mind, is, with elaborate care, excluded. The treatment of prisoners in former times was barbarous, but it was at least intelligent. Its whole purpose was punishment, and the punishment was thorough and drastic. But in this shallow and conceited age we pride ourselves that we are not as our fathers were. Our great aim in prison discipline is the reformation of the offender; and with a stupidity that would be amusing if the matter were not so serious, we wantonly deprive a prisoner of the good influences that God's world of nature is so well fitted to exert upon him. "The heavens declare His glory and the firmament showeth His handiwork;" but our prison cells are specially designed to shut out their testimony; and with the smug Pharisaism so characteristic of the age, we pride ourselves on our philanthropy, and boast of supplying our criminals with goody books, and religion (turned on like the water and the gas), to elevate and reform them.

I am no advocate for pampering and petting a criminal. It is right that the very furniture of his cell and the routine of his daily life should unceasingly impress upon him that crime brings punishment. But to shut him up in a cell where he cannot look out upon land and sky is on a par with flogging him. I would place him in a punishment cell, and flog him too, if he deserved it, and some competent authority directed it. But to make this his daily discipline is unworthy of an enlightened age. I suppose there are men so constituted, or so brutalised, that the want of a window would be a matter of indifference to them. As for myself, I think it would drive me mad.

As it concerns the public to know the causes that lead to inefficiency in the public service, I must here say something more about the Treasury. When I was invited to enter the Home Office I consulted the Irish Attorney-General, not only as to whether I should accede to the wishes of the Government, but also as to the remuneration I should claim. I accepted less than half the amount he specified, because, as Mr. Gathorne Hardy explained to me, my salary would appear in the estimates, and therefore it had to bear comparison with the other salaries of the Office. But when the change of Government occurred, and Mr. Bruce succeeded Mr Hardy as Secretary of State, the Treasury seized the opportunity to reopen the question of my services. Mr. Bruce's reply was that my duties in connection with the Secret Service were of the greatest importance to the Government. Then, said the Treasury, my salary must be charged on the Secret Service Fund. In vain did the Home Office protest that this would be a violation of an express prohibition in the statute regulating the administration of that fund. The Treasury cared nothing for an Act of Parliament if it stood in the way of gratifying their pettifogging meanness towards a public servant. I was extremely indignant, of course, but otherwise I was indifferent; for, as previously mentioned, at that time I intended to return to the Bar. So I contented myself by reopening the question of the amount of my remuneration, and I received an assurance that my pocket would not suffer by the change.

All this was before Mr. Cross when he

offered me the Secretaryship of the Prison Commission.[1] The position, he told me, was not what he had intended, but it was the best the Treasury would allow him to give me, and he would get me something better later on. And in his last year at Whitehall he tried to make good his words, but his efforts only brought a typical Treasury epistle, to the effect that I had "no qualifications beyond what were usually found in the public service." My clerks were the pick of the whole prison service, and so I came down to their level, and no longer attempted anything that they could not do for me. And on these terms I not only secured the friendship of my official chief in the Prison Department, but I became much more free for work of a more important and interesting kind.

No one need suppose that I was personally obnoxious to the Treasury. The whole point of my story is to show how that department demoralises the public service. Its duties in relation to the budget and the revenue may be admirably performed, but its influence in regard to the Government offices is most pernicious. The pay and pension in every department are fixed, and therefore the staff are independent of

[1] See page 79 *ante*.

the Treasury, unless when exceptional circumstances are held to entitle some individual to some special indulgence or favour. And then it is that the Treasury declares itself. Its ways are those of the low-class moneylender who ignores all appeals to justice and fair dealing. There is this difference, however. Treasury officials are gentlemen in private life, and while a poor devil who has no social influence need expect nothing but a snub, anybody who is somebody may possibly get what he wants.

The position which the Home Secretary had claimed for me would have carried with it the right to reckon five or seven years' extra service in computing my pension on retirement. I decided to do still better for myself in this respect. The day of the change of Government in 1880 I went to the Treasury about it and put my case before the Parliamentary Secretary (Sir Henry Ibbetson—afterwards Lord Rookwood). I had come too late, he told me ; he had just received orders to consider himself *functus officio* at four o'clock. At that moment Big Ben struck three ; and playing on the word "minute," I said, "But you have got a whole hour, and I only want a minute." With a laugh he replied that he could not take the initiative in such a matter ; if I had brought him an official letter from the Secretary of State he would gladly have helped me, for he was fully aware of my services to Government. "I'll bring you the letter," I said. I hurried back to the Home Office; and at ten minutes to four o'clock I handed him the letter, and there and then—it was his last official act—he wrote the minute which made my service for pension date from the day of my coming to London in December, 1867.

Let no one dismiss this as mere egotistical gossip. My object is to exemplify the baneful influence of the Treasury in the public service. On a later occasion a visit to the Chancellor of the Exchequer secured for me a much more important benefit than that which I have just described.

CHAPTER VI

Drawn back into Secret Service work by Sir W. Harcourt—1880 an epoch in Ireland—"Boycotting" inaugurated—Mr. Forster's "Suspects Act"—Nature of and necessity for "Coercion Acts"—Meaning of "Secret Service"—Angling for informants: mode in which two were secured—Preventing crimes—Gladstone's Leeds speech of October, 1881—Parnell's contemptuous reply and Gladstone's rejoinder—The "Kilmainham Treaty"—The Premier and Mrs. O'Shea—The Phœnix Park murders—Gladstone's finance and "Free Trade."

Dr. Johnson held that no one but a scoundrel would write except for profit. And a contemporary genius lately declared that it is only donkeys and fools who ever work; but this philosopher propounded his thesis to the unsympathetic ears of a Police Magistrate, who sent him to "hard labour" under the Vagrant Act. Though it is only in late years that I have joined the "unemployed," I have always felt a sneaking sort of agreement with their principles. And though I have never acted on them, I thoroughly believe in idleness—not change of work, but sheer idleness—as a temporary relaxation from work; and I took advantage of the change of Government in 1880 to secure a holiday in the sense of "taking things easy" for a while. The six months that followed were indeed the nearest approach to an adequate holiday that I ever enjoyed in my official life. I was careful not to offend Sir Edmund du Cane by displaying any zeal in the business of his Department, and my deep and growing distaste for Secret Service work led me to contemplate withdrawing from it altogether. As a matter of fact, I had openings for other work, both literary and professional, which would have made me independent of it.

Having these ends in view I refused the usual introduction to the new Secretary of State. But "the best laid plans of mice and men," &c.! On the 3rd of November Sir William Harcourt sent for me. No man could say kinder things than he when in that mood; and telling me that he was fully aware of my past services to Government, he appealed to me to give him the same help I had rendered to his predecessors. He there and then sent for the Commissioner of Police and the head of the Criminal Investigation Department, and bespoke the goodwill of Scotland Yard for me in the duties he was entrusting to me.

Forster's "Suspects Act"

The year 1880 was an epoch-making time in Ireland. Then it was that "boycotting" was inaugurated—that crime which, as one of the Irish judges lately said from the Bench, makes the life of its victim a living death. If taken in hand at once, boycotting might have been easily checked. But once the people were allowed to prove the power of this terrible system of coercion, counter-coercion of a drastic kind was needed to suppress it. And, as Lord Morley's "Life of Gladstone" tells us, any proposal to coerce the lawless who were thus coercing the law-abiding was resisted by the Premier. The magistrates and police were encouraged to do all that was possible under "ordinary law" to check the forces of disorder. But the effort was hopeless, and when Ministers returned to London after the vacation, the Cabinet at last decided to take action.

Parliament met a month earlier than usual (6th of January, 1881), and three weeks afterwards Forster's "Suspects Act," as it was called, was introduced, a statute under which 955 persons were imprisoned under warrants issued by the Lord-Lieutenant. If all the guilty had been arrested under it the arrests would have been tenfold more numerous. For the reported outrages in the preceding year totalled 2,590, and these were only a fraction of the crimes committed. But the guilt of these crimes does not rest mainly upon the peasantry of Ireland. For they were the outcome of persistent incitement by their political leaders, and they were condoned by the Gladstone Government.

Ireland cannot be governed without a "Coercion Act." There have been shameful and disastrous intervals, such as 1880–1882 and 1907–1909, during which the Government of the Crown has been practically suspended in many parts of the country. But government has never been maintained there without "coercion"; and when the legislative Union rescued that unfortunate land from the intolerable evils of "Home Rule," a drastic coercion code, framed in the Irish House of Commons, passed as a legacy to the Imperial Parliament.

A Coercion Act, I should explain, is defined to be a statute which is not a part of the general law, but applies only to some specified portion of the kingdom. And within the limits to which it applies it arms the police with powers unknown to the ordinary law, and sometimes foreign to the spirit of that law. For example, under one leading statute of this character any police constable may call anybody to account whom he finds loitering in any place after sunset. And if the constable considers that the account which the loiterer gives of himself is unsatisfactory, he may arrest him and bring him before a police magistrate, who may send him to hard labour for a month, and this without appeal. If such a law were enforced in disturbed Ireland to-day we should hear very little about cattle-driving!

"Monstrous!" the reader will exclaim. "No free people would ever tolerate such a law," As a matter of fact, seven millions of free people in London tolerate it; for it is a typical clause of the Police Acts under which the Metropolis has been governed for seventy years. There is no great city in the world in which life and property are so safe as in London, and this is largely due to our being governed, not by ordinary law, but by police law. For London, like Ireland, could not be governed without a Coercion Act.

I have been betrayed into this digression by impatience with the claptrap we hear about coercion—"blatherumskite" they call it in Ireland. When I went off the rails I was about to explain that in the year 1880 the immunity enjoyed by agrarian crime in Ireland stimulated the fomentors of political crime; and a revival of Fenian activity on that side of the channel excited the conspirators over here. And it was in these circumstances that Sir William Harcourt re-enlisted me for Secret Service work.

In this country we know nothing of Secret Service in the continental sense of the term. In England the duties thus designated are such as any competent police force would discharge. But with us the expenditure of public money must be open, and subject to audit. In the annual estimates, therefore, a specified amount is taken for Secret Service; and, as regards this fund, the controlling authority must accept a certificate under the hand of a Secretary of State that it is expended for purposes authorised by the statute in that behalf. Were it not for this no Government could obtain information about conspiracies against the State.

Such work was never to my taste, and at this time I had definitely turned away from it. I was still in communication with Major Le Caron and some other prominent American Fenians, but I was out of touch with the leaders of the organisation at home. To ascertain who the London leaders were was an easy task, but how to get hold of them was the problem. They solved that problem for me by forming a plot to discover who their enemy was at Whitehall. A letter came to Whitehall from a man whom I knew by repute as one of the most active and dangerous of the London Fenians. He wished to give information to Government—that was the bait—but he would deal only with "the gentleman at the head of the Intelligence Department." He would hold no communication with the Police.

I met the fellow by appointment one night in a house in Westminster. He lied to me for an hour, during which I listened as though I believed all he was telling me. This, as I expected, led him to ask for money. I then pretended to lose my temper. He had asked to see me in order to give information to Government, and I had come prepared to pay him handsomely, but I was not to be fooled by the yarns he had been giving me. As I spoke I took a handful of sovereigns out of my pocket, and jingled them before him. The greedy look on his face told its own tale. He pleaded that if I would give him time he would tell me all I wished to know, and he meekly asked for his "expenses." I saw that the bait had taken, so I gave him a couple of pounds.

The man made good his promises; but lest he should fail me, I was anxious to get hold of another of the leaders. The London Fenians at this time had copied the American plan of having a public side to the conspiracy; and in furtherance of this scheme they had started a brass band, and the instruments were placed in charge of one of the most trusted of their members. I learned by chance one day that, being "behind with his rent," this fellow had pawned these instruments, and that he was in a state of trepidation owing to their being wanted for an anniversary procession, and he had not money to redeem them. This gave me my chance; and within a few weeks of my being commissioned by the Secretary of State I had the two most influential London Fenians in my pay.

These particulars may be given to-day without breach of confidence, or injury to the public service, and they will explain what Secret Service work means. What grand copy it would have been for the newspapers of that time, if, in describing the Fenian procession that followed, they could have added that the band instruments had been taken out of pawn with money supplied by the Home Office! I will only add that the hold I thus obtained upon the London organisation prevented the commission of Fenian outrages at a critical time; and further, that the information I received from these men was never used to bring a criminal charge against any member of the conspiracy.

To prevent outrages was by no means an easy task; for the Fenians were exasperated by the action of the Government in introducing the "Suspects Act," as it was called, and in arresting Michael Davitt on the forfeiture of his licence.

But I warned the leaders who were in my pay that if outrages occurred I should possibly denounce them and certainly stop their stipends. I use the word "stipend" advisedly. In work of this kind payment by results may operate as a positive incitement to crime, whereas the regular payment of a fixed amount has a marvellous influence on the recipient. He learns to count upon it, and is careful to do nothing to forfeit it. I give my experience for the benefit of others who may hereafter have similar duties to discharge. But I am bound in honesty to add, that if they consult their personal interests they had better not follow my advice. For in Secret Service work, *kudos* is not to be gained by preventing crimes, but by detecting them, and successfully prosecuting the offenders!

These pages are neither biography nor history, and the eventful period ending with the Kilmainham Treaty and the Phœnix Park murder shall receive but passing notice. In his famous Leeds speech of October, 1881, Mr. Gladstone proclaimed that no labouring population in Europe had made such progress as the Irish (a fact which the agitator ignores or denies); but he went on to say that Parnell and the Land League stood between the people and the prosperity which the Land Act would bring them. Parnell was a living proof that the Irish question of the moment was a conflict between law on the one side and lawlessness on the other. But, the Premier declared, "the resources of civilisation are not yet exhausted." This was on Friday, October 7th. Speaking at Wexford on the following Sunday, Parnell launched his reply. He poured contempt and ridicule on Mr. Gladstone's philippic, comparing him to a schoolboy whistling to keep up his courage while passing through a cemetery at night.

Three days later the Cabinet met, and after five hours' discussion it was decided to send Parnell to Kilmainham Gaol under the Suspects Act. The Land League immediately replied by issuing the "No Rent" manifesto, and on the 18th the Government responded by suppressing the League. On the 27th came the great Liverpool oration, in which Mr. Gladstone vehemently denounced the assertion that Parnell "commanded the support of the people of Ireland."

"We are at issue," he exclaimed, "with an organised attempt to override the free will and judgment of the Irish nation. . . . It is a conflict for the very first and elementary principles upon which civil society is constituted. It is idle to talk of either law or order or religion or civilisation if these gentlemen are to carry through the reckless and chaotic scheme they have devised. Rapine is the first object, but rapine is not the only object. These gentlemen wish to march through rapine to the disintegration and dismemberment of the Empire."

What a cynical smile must have lit up Parnell's handsome face as he read this speech in his snug room in Kilmainham! The whistling was growing louder! Six months later the secret treaty of Kilmainham was settled. Mr. Gladstone acknowledged that Parnell and the Land League "commanded the support of the majority of the people of Ireland," and he undertook to promote their policy; and Parnell on his part promised to use his influence to put an end to the outrage campaign, and to give parliamentary support to the Government in "forwarding Liberal principles." And, as Mr. Gladstone declared in the course of the Home Rule debates of 1893, "from that date forward no hard word, and no word of censure, in any speech of mine respecting Mr. Parnell was to be found."

That charming historical romance, the Irish section of Morley's "Life of Gladstone," gives an account of the Kilmainham treaty which, I suppose, will pass into history. The Premier's colleagues in the Cabinet attributed his change of policy to the assurances received through Captain O'Shea, M.P. (the emissary of Lord Morley's story), "that Mr. Parnell was desirous to use his influence on behalf of peace." These assurances were communicated by Mr. Chamberlain to the Cabinet on April 25th; and at the next Council, held that day week, it was decided to release the Irish outrage-mongers and to allow the Act under which they were imprisoned to lapse.

By several of the Ministers that decision was accepted with misgivings. But the author of the Leeds and Liverpool philippics was its staunch and enthusiastic advocate. Of the real grounds on which he supported it his colleagues knew nothing, for until April, 1893, the real Kilmainham treaty was a profound secret. The high contracting parties to that treaty were the Prime Minister on the one side, and on the other the only person on earth who enjoyed the unreserved confidence of the Irish leader. I refer, of course, to Mrs. O'Shea, who afterwards became his wife. And the negotiations took place in a *tête-à-tête* in Thomas's Hotel in Berkeley Square. *Cherchez la femme.* Many a great man has been fooled by a woman!

The Phœnix Park Murders

On Saturday morning, May 6th, Lord Spencer landed in Ireland to inaugurate the new policy which was to bring peace to the country. Just twelve hours later Lord Frederick Cavendish, the newly-appointed Chief Secretary, and Thomas Henry Burke, the Permanent Under-Secretary at Dublin Castle, were murdered in the Phœnix Park. The policy of the Kilmainham treaty, which not a hundred hours before had been deliberately adopted by the Cabinet, was instantly discarded; and not only the British public but the Ministers of the Crown gave themselves up to a fit of blind passion and panic. What wonder is it if English government is despised by the Irish people! If the Cabinet's decision on the Tuesday was right, the murder on the Saturday in no way justified the reversal of it. For however deep might be the responsibility of the Ministry for this crime, Parnell was clear of it; and the horror which it excited in the breast of almost every Irishman would have afforded him the leverage without which he could never have fulfilled his part of the Kilmainham compact.

And real statesmanship would have recognised that Cavendish's murder was an event of no special significance. As a matter of fact it was a mere accident. That the Invincibles had planned the death of Forster, Burke, and my own brother—the Crown Solicitor—was known at Dublin Castle. I myself had given definite warnings of these plots. But Cavendish was a stranger to the assassins, and it was not till after the event that they learned the identity of their second victim. It was indeed a brutal murder; but the criminal returns of the time record a long list of murders quite as brutal and far more significant of the condition of the country. But the savage crimes which marked the rule of the League only led up to the surrender to the League. So long as it was only the Irish who were the victims, Downing Street was callously indifferent. And if poor Tom Burke had been alone that evening, his murder would have been condoned, and the Kilmainham treaty would have stood. And it must in honesty be acknowledged that, if Parnell had been given a free hand, Ireland would have suffered less during the year which followed than it did under Mr. Gladstone's administration.

The Phœnix Park murder was one of the turning-points in my official life. The Secret Service is thankless work, and, moreover, I had never taken to it *con amore*. So in the winter of 1881–2 I again decided to turn from it. This resolution was due in part to offers of work that was more to my taste. One was in the sphere of journalism, a second related to literary work of a higher kind, and the third was professional. A gentleman, whose name looms large in public life, called on me to say that R. S. Wright (afterwards Mr. Justice Wright), who had been advising him in his parliamentary work, was obliged to withdraw his services on account of his receiving a Treasury appointment, and he had recommended me as his successor. I have often been gratified to find how highly I am esteemed by people who don't know me! And here was a signal instance of it, for Wright and I were strangers.

The work I thus undertook was thoroughly compatible with my duties in the Prison Department, and it was altogether congenial. But that hateful and fateful murder drew me back into the toils from which I thought I had escaped; and all that remains to me of that episode in my life is that I made a friendship which I have valued ever since, and that I became inoculated with views about Tariff Reform, which were then deemed not only heretical but eccentric.

In dealing with a legal point relating to taxation, I had occasion to refer to the Budget of the previous session. This led me for private purposes to enter on the study of Gladstone's system of finance, and two discoveries took possession of my mind. First, that in prosperous years Gladstone drew his pen through entire pages of the tariff list, simply because the money was not needed. And secondly, that in numerous cases the remission of taxation brought no benefit to the public, and in various instances it proved an embarrassment even to the trades affected by it; for they had been used to accept Customs measurements for trade purposes, and the remission involved them in expense which, in some cases, nearly equalled the amount of the duty.

Here are some facts which merit prominence to-day. First, that Mr. Gladstone reduced the number of articles taxed at the Customs from 1163 to 48. Secondly, that of the amount now received annually from the Customs some £13,500,000 come from taxes on food, and chiefly on tea and sugar, which are necessaries of life to the poorest of the poor. Thirdly, this means that in the interval since Gladstone's day many hundreds of taxable imports have year after year entered the country free, while hundreds of millions of pounds sterling have been levied on the food of the people. And fourthly—the strangest part of all—this is called "Free Trade"! The English have no sense of humour. What wonder is it that the Irish think them a stupid people!

CHAPTER VII

Government action after the Phœnix Park murders—Col. Brackenbury's appointment at Dublin Castle—Gladstone's Coercion Act—The Explosive Substances Act, 1883—The Dublin prosecutions—Policy of scare and panic: Mrs. Roundell's diary—A Sunday morning's experiences—Sir W. Harcourt's "dynamite moods"—Some typical incidents—Snubbing his colleagues—The Queen's Jubilee dynamite plot—Mr. Monro's action.

I HAVE recorded how, as the result of a prolonged struggle, and at the cost of dismissing two of its members, the great see-saw Government of the eighties adopted a new Irish policy one Tuesday afternoon, and how an incident which occurred upon the following Saturday led to a complete reversal of that deliberate and grave decision. During the eighty years that had elapsed since the Union, Westminster had been content to draw upon the old Irish enactments framed in College Green, whenever the Irish got out of hand and needed special legislation to restrain them. But now a new Coercion Act was devised, such as even the Irish Home Rule Parliament had never dreamed of.[1] And special measures were adopted to administer it. An "Under Secretaryship for Police and Crime" was established at Dublin Castle, and Colonel (now General Sir Henry) Brackenbury was appointed to the office. In due course he appealed to me to represent his department in London. I twice refused in the most definite way to accept his overtures; but at last, under pressure from Sir William Harcourt, I had to comply. My position was a delicate one; for being in the public service, I could not well make my private engagements a ground for refusing to undertake public duties. The remuneration offered me was liberal, and it was a pleasure to work with him. But his tenure of the post was brief; for when Lord Wolseley's Egyptian expedition was launched, a longing for military duty took possession of him, and he left the Castle.

The story of the eventful years that followed

[1] True it is, as averred by Lady Frederick Cavendish in a recent letter to the *Times*, that a Coercion Bill was drafted prior to the murders. As a matter of fact, the question before the Cabinet had been the adoption of this Bill or, as an alternative, of the "Kilmainham Treaty." But after the murders the Bill was strengthened by new clauses unknown in previous legislation of the kind.

is matter of history, and I am not writing history. I have special reasons, moreover, for dealing lightly with that story. This much I would say, that while the principal events of the Fenian dynamite campaign of a quarter of a century ago are known, even to the generation that has grown up since then, very few people appreciate the labours by which that campaign was crushed and its emissaries were brought to justice. There is but one way by which crime can be suppressed, and that is by coercion, for every criminal statute is a "Coercion Act." And while in dealing with crime in Ireland the Legislature allows itself to be fooled by sentimental objections and clap-trap, no drivel of that kind gets a hearing when crime in England is in question. And so, when the dynamiters began their fiendish work, "ordinary law" was discarded, and a most extraordinary statute—Sir William Harcourt's Explosive Substances Act, 1883—was hurried through Parliament, with the result that the crime against which it was aimed was soon stamped out.

But for the English Coercion Act very few of the dynamiters could have been convicted. But for the Irish Coercion Act the Phœnix Park murderers would all have escaped the gallows. The English Act remains in force, and for a quarter of a century we have had no dynamiting.

These Irish Acts are allowed to lapse, and the outrage campaign is from time to time resumed.

I had no part whatever in the Dublin prosecutions. They were admirably conducted, and the chief credit for their success was due to my brother, the late Sir Samuel Lee Anderson, then Acting Crown Solicitor at the Castle, and Mr. J. A. Curran, now a County Court Judge, but then a Dublin police magistrate, who conducted an inquiry under a clause of the Act which authorised a Court to take evidence upon oath without the presence of any person charged with crime. I may here add the interesting fact that the first clue to the guilty men was a chance remark, dropped by one of the witnesses, about "a car with a white horse."

Although Colonel Brackenbury's leaving Ireland involved no immediate change in my duties, it sensibly lessened my pleasure in discharging them. I had neither responsibility for, nor sympathy with, the senseless and baneful policy of scare and panic that marked the years of Sir George Trevelyan's term of office as Chief Secretary. Not only were he and the Viceroy thus victimised, but also the ladies of the Viceregal Court. The following extract from Mrs. Charles S. Roundell's diary describes how they used to take an airing in those days:—

"After luncheon Lady Spencer asked me to drive in state with her. We drove in a barouche and four, with postillions and outriders. An A.D.C. sat opposite to us with his revolver in his hand under the fur rug. Two footmen sat in the rumble behind, each wearing a powerful whistle hung round his neck by a red cord, and with pistols in a holster by his side. There followed two mounted soldiers with drawn swords in their hands and pistols in their holsters. In this fashion we drove through some of the principal streets of Dublin." [1]

Even when the Invincibles were on the prowl, these ladies might have driven, or even walked, alone through any street in Dublin. I knew all that was doing over there; but I kept to my own duties in London, and held my peace.

My work at Whitehall was many-sided. I continued to discharge my functions on the Prison Commission to the full satisfaction of my official chief in that department,[2] I was retained by the Irish Government to look after their interests in London, and I had also a retaining fee from the Secretary of State in relation to political crime generally. Taking my Civil Service salary into

[1] The *Nineteenth Century*, October, 1906.

[2] See p. 80, *ante*.

account, my remuneration was reasonably adequate. But it was not easily earned ; and when the dynamite campaign began, my position was by no means a sinecure. I was in daily communication with Dublin Castle, and I kept up a private correspondence with our consuls in New York and other American cities, as well as with Le Caron and my other American informants. And never a week passed without my having to meet London informants, sometimes at my residence, and sometimes at out-of-the-way places—for of course they never came to Whitehall.

A glance at my old diaries reminds me of many an arduous and anxious day's work. But I am not so egotistical as to suppose the details would be of interest to others. I will give one day's engagements, however, as a specimen. On coming out of church one Sunday morning (February 18, 1883) I found a police constable in uniform, with a hansom cab, awaiting me. He had been sent to fetch me to a conference at Sir William Harcourt's house. That a gentleman should be arrested on leaving church on a Sunday morning, and driven to the lock-up in a hansom is a rare event, and this was evidently the view taken by those of the onlookers who did not know who I was.

The Irish Government had called for the arrest

of the wife of Frank Byrne, the League official who had provided the knives for the murderers of Cavendish and Burke ; and Sir William, as was his wont, summoned every one who could say anything bearing on the case. The Under Secretary of State, Howard Vincent and myself were caught, and responded. After our consultation, Vincent and I drove to Westminster and made the needed arrangements. Later in the afternoon I was again summoned to Scotland Yard, the woman and her sister-in-law having been brought in. Then, after tea at the Savile Club, I made for Chelsea, where I had promised to address a meeting. After supper that evening I felt that I had done a fair day's work, and I sat down to enjoy my arm-chair till bed-time. But about half-past eleven o'clock one of my satellites arrived to tell me that another of the League women had come from Dublin, with money from the League Treasurer to enable the fugitive criminals of the League, who were then in France, to escape to America. I drove to Grosvenor Square, and having knocked up Howard Vincent, I put the case in his hands. But he coaxed me into relieving him of the job, and letting him go back to bed. So on I went to Scotland Yard, empowered to. represent him for the night.

Coursing hares or shooting birds is fool's play

compared with work of this sort, and I was so keen that I went out with the officers whom I entrusted with the case. But when I got home again at 3 a.m. I had taken nothing except the most uncommon catarrh I ever had in my life! As I afterwards ascertained, my information was perfectly accurate. The woman was in the house we were watching. But she slept there, instead of returning to her hotel as she had intended to do. Had she come out during the night, we should have seized that money. But the facts did not warrant our breaking into the house, and so I was baffled. In my Irish book I tell how grievously I suffered in Sir William Harcourt's good opinion because of my failure.

Though I say this, my relations with him were pleasant, and I had many proofs of his kindness. He had what Du Cane used to call his "dynamite moods" at times; but they were as brief as they were disagreeable, and I never served under any one to whom I could speak with so little reserve. I was always free of his room both at Whitehall and at his residence; and while he was never annoyed by my coming to him, he sometimes resented my staying away. At one time, while the dynamite scare was acute, I deliberately kept out of his way until specially summoned to 7, Grafton Street. When I entered the room of the mythical round table —there was no round table in it—he ignored my salutation and his first words were, "Mr. Anderson, it's three weeks since you were last in this room." When Sir William called me "Mr. Anderson," it was a clear case of "Stand from under"; but after a while he sat down in one of his arm-chairs, motioning me to the other, and in his genial way he kept me talking with him for half an hour.

I had many similar experiences. And while most men resent being proved in the wrong, he never did. The day following one of the dynamite explosions he summoned me to Grafton Street, and read to me a long and elaborate minute he had prepared, apportioning my own duties and those of Scotland Yard in relation to Fenian work. He got very angry when I told him it wouldn't do, and he accused me of wishing to thwart him. But after a while we were seated in the arm-chairs, which stood on either side of the fireplace; and forty minutes later he tore up the paper to which I objected, and, in dismissing me, desired me to come to his room at the House of Commons that afternoon.

Sir William Harcourt's "dynamite moods" were not reserved for his subordinates. I might cite many incidents in proof of this, but one must suffice. When sent for one day on his return from a Cabinet Council, I found Lord Northbrook and Mr. Forster with him. A dispatch had been received from Washington, he told me, reporting a serious dynamite plot, and asking for instructions relative to an offer from one of the parties to betray his co-conspirators on certain specified conditions. He gave me in a few words the substance of the dispatch, warning me that it was most secret, no one outside the Cabinet having seen it; but they wished to have my advice upon it.

The Chief Secretary was perambulating the room; and the First Lord of the Admiralty, who was seated by the fireplace with the dispatch in his hand, had evidently been holding forth upon it when I entered. He resumed his say; but before he had got far, Sir William snatched the paper from him, much as a quick-tempered teacher might treat a schoolboy, and handing it to me, he said in a petulant way, "There, Anderson, what do you think we ought to do?" I did not tell him that I had read it that morning in the Secretary of State's room at the Foreign Office; but I quietly re-perused it, and then expressed the opinion I had formed upon it. "Quite right," said he; and without another word to his colleagues, my chief took up his pen and proceeded to minute the paper, muttering as he did so something about "people who don't understand." Lord Northbrook and Mr. Forster walked out of the room. Is it strange that when his chance came to succeed to the Premiership his former colleagues refused to serve under him?

The acceptance of the informant's offer would have made us practically a party to the intended crime; for the first payment which he claimed for his information would have been used for the furtherance of the plot. No agent of the British Government would become intentionally an *agent-provocateur;* but in those days it needed both vigilance and shrewdness to avoid blundering into a false position which would have involved that reproach.

Such a case occurred in 1887. There was a hellish plot to bring about a dynamite explosion in Westminster Abbey during the historic ceremony of Queen Victoria's Jubilee, and one of the principal agents in that plot was taken into pay on behalf of our Government. But the scheme was discovered and thwarted by Mr. Monro, then Assistant Commissioner of Police, who most fortunately had at that time been placed in charge of the Secret Service work. The arrangement had been made during a disastrous interval before his appointment; and he had no knowledge of it until a prominent Fenian—I will here call him Jinks—arrived at Boulogne to carry out his twofold mission on behalf of the American Clan-na-Gael and the British Government. He brought his wife to Europe with him and posed as a tourist. Ex-Superintendent Thomson of Bow Street, who had formerly served in the detective department at Scotland Yard, was at once sent to Boulogne, and he put up at the hotel where Jinks was staying. He too had his wife with him; and as the women struck up a friendship, the men soon came together. When Mr. Monro had gained full knowledge of the plot he sent Superintendent (afterwards Chief Constable) Williamson to Boulogne to deal with Jinks. The man was notified that the bargain made with him was now repudiated, and he was warned against crossing the Channel.

Police work has often a humorous side to it, and the situation here was amusing. Williamson sat down at the same table with Jinks and Thomson; the ex-Superintendent posing as a stranger to his former chief and colleague in the police, and hobnobbing with the Fenian whom he had come to watch, and possibly to denounce. Williamson was on tenterhooks lest Mrs. Thomson should "give away the whole show"; but she fulfilled her part admirably; and Jinks went back to America in ignorance of the counterplot of which he had been the victim.

But those who were watching events were in no mood just then to appreciate the humour of the piece. The situation was extremely grave, and gave cause for deep anxiety. It was known that the subordinate agents of the plot were here, but the police were unable to trace them. The danger was lest, on finding that they were deserted by their chief, they should act on their own account. The hope was that, left to themselves, they would remain inactive. The fear was falsified and the hope fulfilled.

To have carried out the original scheme, and to have seized these men and brought them to justice, letting the agent who betrayed them return to New York with his pockets lined with English gold—this would have been ostensibly a brilliant police coup, but it would have been achieved by discreditable means. On the other hand, an outrage in the Abbey at the Jubilee service would have been a disaster of such magnitude that some might think any means legitimate to avert it. *Fiat justitia, ruat cœlum*, is a pagan maxim. The Christian version of it is, fearlessly to do the right and trust to an overruling Providence. But it needed a strong man to accept the risks, and such a man was then at the helm. But he never received the credit which was his due, for the public knew nothing of what I have here detailed.

Men engaged in work of this kind do not indulge in hysterical emotion. But I remember as though it happened yesterday my visit to Monro on that eventful day, after the Queen had reached the Palace and the Abbey guests had scattered. The intense anxiety of many days was at an end, and we gripped each other by the hand without a word from either of us.

CHAPTER VIII

Sir A. Liddell's friendship and his death — Dishonourable treatment—Appeal to Sir W. Harcourt: his generosity and kindness—The Criminal Investigation Department created in 1878 under Howard Vincent—Succeeded by Mr. Monro under Sir C. Warren—Bickerings with the Home Office—Personal notes—The Police Pension Act.

On a previous page I have told how largely my decision to remain at the Home Office was influenced by the personality of the Under Secretary of State; and Sir Adolphus Liddell's death in June, 1885, was a cruel blow to me. Before I moved from the Irish Office to Whitehall, in April, 1868, I had already gained his friendship, and for the next seventeen years I was as free of his room as if I had been the house cat. And during all those years his friendship for me never flagged, never altered, and I never had a tiff with him.

Yes, on one occasion I made him angry; and that once he spoke to me in a way that wounded me. Fearing lest a king might arise to whom Joseph might be unknown, I asked him to write a minute, putting on record his estimate of my services and my claims on Government. Himself the soul of honour, he indignantly resented the suggestion that any Secretary of State would act dishonourably toward a public servant; and when I pressed my appeal, he lost his temper with me. But after the change of Government in February, 1886, my fears of dishonourable treatment were fully realised by the action of Mr. Childers and the new permanent Under Secretary. It was intimated to me that, apart from my Prison Commission appointment, my services were no longer required, and that, as I had been paid for those services, I had no further claims on Government. Although my feeling of indignation at such treatment exceeded my sense of the pecuniary loss it involved, I decided to make a personal appeal to the Chancellor of the Exchequer to deliver me out of the hands of my own chief.

When I called at the Treasury Sir William Harcourt received me at once, as he had been used to do in his Home Office days, and I shall never forget his kind words and generous sympathy when I told him of my trouble. He then and there wrote a letter to Childers about me, which he most kindly allowed me to read. But his help did not end there. Having "the power of the purse," he saved me from the money loss which the scandalous action of the Home Secretray would have entailed on me. It was with confidence that I appealed to him. Owing to influences at which I have already hinted, I was "in his black books" during his last weeks at the Home Office, and I saw him very seldom. But some time after he left Whitehall, I had a kind note, asking me to call at Grafton Street. He received me as cordially as of old, and told me in plain words that, since leaving office, he had heard things which led him to appreciate more highly the advice and help I had given him, and the policy I had always advocated. In a word, had he been my equal he could not have made a more gracious *amende* for his unfair treatment of me. I sometimes forgive an injury, but I never forget a kindness; is it strange that, ignoring his faults, I remember his noble qualities and cherish his memory?

Mr. Childers' tenure of the Home Office was happily brief, and when Mr. Matthews succeeded him in the following August, I found myself once more holding confidential relations with the department. For, in undertaking the oversight of Secret Service work, Mr. Monro, the Assistant

Commissioner of Police, stipulated upon having my assistance. This arrangement, moreover, drew me into still closer touch with Scotland Yard, and was no doubt one of the many elements which led to my appointment as head of the Criminal Investigation Department in 1888.

That department was created in 1878 as the result of an inquiry by a Home Office Committee, appointed in consequence of certain abuses and irregularities which had come to light in a recent criminal trial. Till then the detective department of the Metropolitan Police, which had been founded in a humble way in 1842, was merely a branch of the Commissioner's office. This system was possible in Sir Richard Mayne's time,[1] for Mayne was a man whose energy equalled his capacity, and he was at home in every branch of police work. But the policeman element was wanting in the personality of his successor. For though Sir Edmund Henderson was a man of marked ability, the success of his administration as Commissioner of Police was due mainly to the respect and confidence he inspired. He never took to the details of police work, and least of all to thief-catching.[2]

[1] See p. 20, *ante*.

[2] During the ten years preceding the reorganisation of the detective branch under Howard Vincent, its success was

I have told how the Home Office refused to make a scapegoat of Mayne at the time of the Clerkenwell explosion fiasco; but Childers was a man of a different type from Gathorne Hardy, and one of his first official acts as Home Secretary was to call the Commissioner of Police to account for the West End riot of February 8, 1886, when a mob collected in Trafalgar Square and made its way to Hyde Park, breaking windows and looting shops *en route*. Henderson resigned, and Sir Charles Warren was appointed in his place.

The first arrangements made upon the report of the Departmental Committee of 1877 ignored some of its principal recommendations.[1] The scheme was that the detective branch should be a separate department under an Assistant Commissioner, who should hold rank next to the Chief Commissioner, and have charge of the whole Force in his absence. But when the Criminal Investigation Department was first con-

mainly due to Frederick Williamson—once known to most Londoners, but now almost forgotten—who was at that time Superintendent at Scotland Yard, and who afterwards became Chief Constable of the Criminal Investigation Department.

[1] It was a "strong" Committee. Sir Henry Selwyn Ibbetson, the Parliamentary Under Secretary of State, was the Chairman, and his colleagues were Colonel the Hon. William Feilding, and Messrs. Overend and Maule, Q.C.'s.

stituted, it was placed under a "Director," who had neither a statutory position nor disciplinary powers. And the fact that this arrangement did not break down within a twelvemonth is a notable testimony to the personality of my friend Howard Vincent. I do not know another man who could have made it succeed.

It was not till Vincent left Scotland Yard that statutory authority was obtained to appoint a third Assistant Commissioner; and under the Metropolitan Police Act, 1884, Mr. Monro was appointed to take charge of the detective department. His appointment marked an epoch in Police administration in London; but the good which ought to have resulted from it was largely hindered by the bickerings which, after a time, began between him and the Chief Commissioner. And those bickerings were aggravated by Sir Charles Warren's relations with the Home Office. As several of the men concerned are still with us, I cannot speak freely on this subject. But this much I may say, that if Sir Adolphus Liddell had been still in office, and the influence of Whitehall had savoured of a plaister rather than of a blister, the course of events would have been different. The result was that Mr. Monro resigned. But London's loss was my gain, for I succeeded to the office.

Mr. Monro's place was not easily filled, and the matter was dealt with by a Committee of the Cabinet. The Departmental Committee of 1877 stipulated that the head of the detective department should be a criminal lawyer; and the obvious importance of this was now recognised. Mr. Monro had given valuable assistance to the Irish Government in relation to political crime; and Mr. A. J. Balfour, who was then Chief Secretary, urged that his successor should be qualified to render similar service. Of course it was essential to have a man who would work harmoniously with the Chief Commissioner, and Sir Charles Warren had said more than once that "if Anderson were at Scotland Yard all would go smoothly." On an earlier page I have spoken of my capacity for imposing on people who don't know me; and here was another proof of it, for Sir Charles and I were practically strangers. The names and claims of a number of men were duly considered; and by a process of "negative induction," it appeared that I was the only man who possessed all the necessary qualifications.

Sir Charles Warren's appointment to the head of the Force was a risky experiment. The Police cannot tolerate military discipline, and this was their first experience of a military Chief Commissioner. For it is no disparagement of Sir

Edmund Henderson to say that he was more of a civilian than a soldier ; and, moreover, he came to Scotland Yard from Whitehall, where he had been at the head of the Prison Department. The effect was precisely what might have been anticipated. I speak with knowledge such as few others possessed, and I can say with definiteness that there was a dangerous want of sympathy between the Commissioner and the rank and file ; and Sir Charles Warren was not the man to make things smoother in such a case. There is no doubt that sedition was smouldering throughout the Force, and serious trouble might have resulted. But a change of sentiment was brought about in a most unlooked-for way. When, with his proverbial boldness, Sir Charles Warren stood forward to defend the Force against the unjust strictures of the Home Office upon the action of the police on the occasion of the Trafalgar Square riots of November, 1887, his faults were condoned ; and by the time that I became his colleague, ten months later, his popularity with the uniformed Force was established.

I may here say at once that, though I was warned by many, including officers who had served under him in South Africa, that "I could never get on with Warren," my relations with

Sir Charles were always easy and pleasant. During all my official life I never failed to "get on" with any man, no matter what his moods, if only he was honourable and straight. I was told that he had a dog-like nature. But I am of that breed myself. I always found him perfectly frank and open, and he treated me as a colleague, leaving me quite unfettered in the control of my department; and when his imperious temper could no longer brook the nagging Home Office ways of that period, and he decided to resign his office, I felt sincere regret at his going. But no one may justly charge me with fickleness and duplicity if I add that my regret gave place to feelings of pleasure when the unexpected followed, and Mr. Monro came back to Scotland Yard as Chief Commissioner.

My satisfaction with the new appointment was by no means based on personal grounds only. If we had been left together for half a dozen years, his administration would have made a permanent mark upon the criminal statistics of the Metropolis. Sir Richard Mayne was thoroughly sympathetic toward detective police work, but he had no proper staff. And during the first ten years of the "C.I.D." the Chief Commissioners were men who were out of touch with work of that kind. But now at last we had a thoroughly efficient detective Force, and a Chief Commissioner who had himself done much to make it what it was, and who had both acquaintance and sympathy with its duties. He told me, indeed more than once, that he sometimes wished himself back in his old chair. And I traded upon this at first by referring specially difficult cases to him. But this he vetoed, telling me plainly that he was not going to do my work for me. But he added in his genial way that the oftener I came to him as a friend to talk over my cases the better he would be pleased.

But it was not to be. His predecessor had been driven out by the Home Office, and he soon yielded to the same influence. I am anticipating events, for I have something to say about my first year at Scotland Yard; but I wish to deal once for all with these personal elements. If Sir Adolphus Liddell had still been Under Secretary of State, Sir Charles Warren and Mr. Monro would have been friends. And with Liddell at Whitehall there would have been no fatal friction between the Commissioner of Police and the Home Secretary. In each case there were two sides to the quarrel. That is a matter of course. But, to repeat my inelegant simile, where a plaister is needed the effect of a blister is intolerable; and but for the blister Mr. Matthews and Mr. Monro might have made *bon ménage*, as the French phrase it. With his many excellent qualities Godfrey Lushington's intervention and influence as Under Secretary were generally provocative, and his manner was irritating.

To show how grotesquely Mr. Monro was misjudged at Whitehall, I may mention that when he summoned the Superintendents to a private conference on the Police Pension Bill he was suspected of a design to foment sedition, and an appeal was made to me confidentially to watch the proceedings.

It is chiefly by the Pension Act that he will be remembered in the Force. Under that statute a police officer can claim a pension after twenty-five years' service; and after twenty-six years he can retire on a full pension of two-thirds of his pay. Formerly a medical certificate was necessary to enable an officer to retire on pension before the ordinary Civil Service age limit was reached. But experience proved that, after twenty-five years of ordinary police duty on the streets, a man might be practically worn out, though organically sound. And on this fact the new scheme was framed. But owing, it may be, to special vigour, or to having been employed on special duties, many a constable is perfectly fit after twenty-five or twenty-six years' service; and in the higher ranks the duties, though of course more responsible, are generally less wearing. It was assumed, however, that the serious financial sacrifice involved in resigning from the Force (and any one can judge what it means to lose a third of his income) would be sufficient to deter officers from making an undue use of their pension rights. And if that assumption has been falsified, it is not those who framed the measure who should be held responsible for the inordinate charges which, in its operation, it has imposed upon the ratepayers of the Metropolis and the public purse.[1]

[1] The amount of these charges may be estimated from the statistics given in the report for 1907. Of the 17,907 officers serving at the end of that year, there were only 85 under the rank of Superintendent who had more than twenty-six years' service. And the proportion of those who stampede after twenty-five years may be gauged from the fact that the corresponding number of those who had served more than twenty-five years was only 219, about one in eighty of the Force.

CHAPTER IX.

First days at Scotland Yard—The "Whitechapel murders"—The criminal a Polish Jew—Demoralisation of the C.I.D. in 1888—Statistics of crime in London—"Undiscovered murders"—The working of the Police machine—Area and population of the Metropolitan Police District—Sir Robert Peel's scheme — Powers of constables — Status of the Commissioners.

MY last chapter brought down my story to my appointment, in September, 1888, as Assistant Commissioner of Police and head of the Criminal Investigation Department. Mr. Monro was not "an easy man to follow," and my difficulties in succeeding to the post were increased by the foolish ways of the Home Office, as well as by the circumstances of the times. As I have already said, Sir Charles Warren had then secured the loyal support of the Force generally. But the officers of the Criminal Investigation Department were demoralised by the treatment accorded to their late chief; and during the interval since his practical retirement sinister rumours were in circulation as to the appointment of his successor. If the announcement had been made that, on his official retirement on the 31st of August, I should succeed to the office, things might have settled down. For all the principal officers knew and trusted me. But for some occult reason the matter was kept secret, and I was enjoined not to make my appointment known. I had been in the habit of frequenting Mr. Monro's room, as we were working together in political crime matters; but when I did so now, and Sir Charles Warren took advantage of my visit to come over to see me, it was at once inferred that he was spying on me because I was Mr. Monro's friend. The indignation felt by the officers was great, and I had some difficulty in preventing Chief-Superintendent Williamson from sending in his resignation.

Then, again, I was at that time physically unfit to enter on the duties of my new post. For some time past I had not had an adequate holiday, and the strain of long and anxious work was telling on me. "A man is as old as he feels," and by this test I was older at that time than when I left office a dozen years later. Dr. Gilbart Smith, of Harley Street, insisted that I must have two months' complete rest, and he added that he would probably give me a certificate for a further two months' "sick leave." This, of course, was out of the question. But I told Mr. Matthews, greatly to his distress, that I could not take up my new duties until I had had a month's holiday in Switzerland. And so, after one week at Scotland Yard, I crossed the Channel.

But this was not all. The second of the crimes known as the Whitechapel murders was committed the night before I took office, and the third occurred the night of the day on which I left London. The newspapers soon began to comment on my absence. And letters from Whitehall decided me to spend the last week of my holiday in Paris, that I might be in touch with my office. On the night of my arrival in the French capital two more victims fell to the knife of the murder-fiend; and next day's post brought me an urgent appeal from Mr. Matthews to return to London; and of course I complied.

On my return I found the Jack-the-Ripper scare in full swing. When the stolid English go in for a scare they take leave of all moderation and common sense. If nonsense were solid, the nonsense that was talked and written about those murders would sink a *Dreadnought*. The subject is an unsavoury one, and I must write about it with reserve. But it is enough to say that the wretched victims belonged to a very small class of degraded women who frequent the East End streets after midnight, in hope of inveigling belated drunkards, or men as degraded as themselves. I spent the day of my return to town, and half the following night, in reinvestigating the whole case, and next day I had a long conference on the subject with the Secretary of State and the Chief Commissioner of Police. "We hold you responsible to find the murderer," was Mr. Matthews' greeting to me. My answer was to decline the responsibility. "I hold myself responsible," I said, "to take all legitimate means to find him." But I went on to say that the measures I found in operation were, in my opinion, wholly indefensible and scandalous; for these wretched women were plying their trade under definite Police protection. Let the Police of that district, I urged, receive orders to arrest every known "street woman" found on the prowl after midnight, or else let us warn them that the Police will not protect them. Though the former course would have been merciful to the very small class of women affected by it, it was deemed too drastic, and I fell back on the second.

However the fact may be explained, it is a fact that no other street murder occurred in the

"Jack-the-Ripper" series.[1] The last and most horrible of that maniac's crimes was committed in a house in Miller's Court on the 9th of November. And the circumstances of that crime disposed of all the theories of the amateur "Sherlock Holmeses" of that date.

One did not need to be a Sherlock Holmes to discover that the criminal was a sexual maniac of a virulent type; that he was living in the immediate vicinity of the scenes of the murders; and that, if he was not living absolutely alone, his people knew of his guilt, and refused to give him up to justice. During my absence abroad the Police had made a house-to-house search for him, investigating the case of every man in the district whose circumstances were such that he could go and come and get rid of his blood-stains in secret. And the conclusion we came to was that he and his people were certain low-class Polish Jews; for it is a remarkable fact that

[1] I am here assuming that the murder of Alice M'Kenzie on the 17th of July, 1889, was by another hand. I was absent from London when it occurred, but the Chief Commissioner investigated the case on the spot and decided that it was an ordinary murder, and not the work of a sexual maniac. And the Poplar case of December, 1888, was a death from natural causes, and but for the "Jack the Ripper" scare, no one would have thought of suggesting that it was a homicide.

people of that class in the East End will not give up one of their number to Gentile justice.

And the result proved that our diagnosis was right on every point. For I may say at once that "undiscovered murders" are rare in London, and the "Jack-the-Ripper" crimes are not within that category. And if the Police here had powers such as the French Police possess, the murderer would have been brought to justice. Scotland Yard can boast that not even the subordinate officers of the department will tell tales out of school, and it would ill become me to violate the unwritten rule of the service. So I will only add here that the "Jack-the-Ripper" letter which is preserved in the Police Museum at New Scotland Yard is the creation of an enterprising London journalist.

Having regard to the interest attaching to this case, I am almost tempted to disclose the identity of the murderer and of the pressman who wrote the letter above referred to. But no public benefit would result from such a course, and the traditions of my old department would suffer. I will merely add that the only person who had ever had a good view of the murderer unhesitatingly identified the suspect the instant he was confronted with him; but he refused to give evidence against him.

The Criminal a Polish Jew

In saying that he was a Polish Jew I am merely stating a definitely ascertained fact. And my words are meant to specify race, not religion. For it would outrage all religious sentiment to talk of the religion of a loathsome creature whose utterly unmentionable vices reduced him to a lower level than that of the brute.

In the introduction to the "Scarlet Letter," Hawthorne apologises for his work, on the ground that his position in the Custom House was not a haven of rest. And no one would thus describe the post of head of the Criminal Investigation Department, even in the most peaceful of times. But when I took charge at the close of 1888 the state of things was disquieting and depressing in the extreme. There is a strong *esprit de corps* in the department, and the officers, one and all, felt that their late chief had been unfairly treated. The "Detective Department," moreover, has always been an object of jealousy in the Force, and this disturbing element was specially felt during 1887 and 1888. This appeared very plainly in the Commissioner's Report for 1887: it ignored the Criminal Investigation Department altogether. "Boots are a matter of great concern," the report declared, and it recorded that truncheon pockets had been substituted for truncheon cases; but not one word did it contain about the crime of the Metropolis. Now, unfortunately, neither Mr. Monro nor his successor could ever realise that such matters as boots and truncheon cases, important though they may be, are not as important as the prevention and detection of crime, and the subordinate officers were equally dull-witted. And the efficiency of the Criminal Investigation Department work, unlike ordinary Police duties, cannot but be impaired by influences which discourage or demoralise the staff. The crime returns for 1887 gave proof of this; and it was still more apparent in the following year. The Commissioner's report for 1888 accordingly recorded that "crime during the year has shown a decided tendency to increase."

Such, then, was the state of affairs when I entered on my new duties. And I did not then know, what I afterwards learned, that the Home Office very soon threatened to call me to account because there was not an immediate change. But Sir Charles Warren "put down his foot with a firm hand" (as the Irishman phrased it), and would not allow any interference with me till I had had time to bring matters round. And the Commissioner's report for 1889 announced that "the criminal returns for the year showed a marked improvement upon the statistics for 1888." Still more satisfactory was the report for the following year, which announced "that there was greater security for person and property in the Metropolis during 1890 than in any previous year included in the statistical returns."

Qui s'excuse s'accuse. But I have no need to offer any defence of my reign at Scotland Yard; and it is not in that sense, but as a tribute to the Police Force, and for the satisfaction of the public, that I give the following statistical table, taken from the Commissioner's report for 1898. It shows at a glance what marked success attended the work of the Criminal Investigation Department during the first twenty years of its history. The figures give the average proportion of crimes against property, to each 1,000 of the estimated population of the Metropolis, during the quinquennial periods specified.

1879–1883	...	...	4,856
1884–1888	...	...	3,823
1889–1893	...	...	3,249
1894–1898	...	...	2,755

The proportion for 1899 was 2,439, and for 1900 (my last completed year at Scotland Yard),

2,534.[1] In judging of these results, moreover, it must be remembered that, from 1879 to 1900, the population of the Metropolis increased by some 2,000,000. No other large city in the world could show such results as these. And having regard to the huge population of London, and its peculiar characteristics, the safety of life in the Metropolis is a standing miracle.

One evening in the year after the Chicago Exhibition, I dined with some American gentlemen at the Hotel Cecil, and they gave me some astounding particulars of the number of homicides in that city. They mentioned 2,000 cases as having occurred in the previous year. I can scarcely believe such a tale, but that is not the point of my story. Presently they asked me how many murders we had in London in a year. I pleaded that London was three times as large as Chicago, and that facilities for crime increased in proportion to population : How many cases would they consider normal? After some discussion among themselves, the estimate they gave me was 200. I told them that the preceding year was the worst I had known, as we had twenty murders; but the average was fifteen or sixteen. They threw down

[1] I may add that under the reign of my successor this low average has been maintained.

knives and forks, and stared at me and at each other. My words travelled across the Atlantic, and I received several letters, including one from a prominent official in Washington, asking me if I had spoken seriously and by the book.

Though the Metropolitan Police deserve their meed of praise for such results as these, a full explanation of them must be sought in the characteristics of our national life, and in the peculiar influences to which those characteristics are mainly due.[1] But here I will deal only with the facts. In reply to questions in Parliament last year, the Home Secretary gave the following striking statistics. The murders in the Metropolis, he said, from the 1st of January, 1903, to the 30th of September, 1908, numbered 92, and among these there were only 10 "undiscovered crimes." Four of the 10, moreover, were deaths due to illegal operations; and such cases are murders only in a technical sense. This means six "undiscovered murders," or an average of one per annum, and this in a population that averaged more than 7,000,000 during the six years in question. It seems almost incredible, and I own that I should refuse to believe it if I had not personal knowledge of the care and

[1] See p. 275, *post*.

accuracy with which the criminal statistics are compiled.

And Mr. Herbert Gladstone added that, in some of the cases where no one was made amenable, the criminals were known to the Police, but evidence to justify an arrest was not obtainable. One of the 1908 murder cases, for example, was in this category, both the witnesses and the victim being low-class Polish Jews. This element, I may add, of offences by aliens against aliens, is not a negligible one in considering the crime of London. And even among our own people it sometimes happens that the murderer is known, but evidence is wholly wanting. In such circumstances the French Police would arrest the suspected person, and build up a case against him at their leisure, mainly by admissions extracted from him in repeated interrogations.

I recall a case in which I allowed myself to be goaded by popular clamour into taking a first step in French procedure. It was a murder that excited unusual interest, and the murderer, a near relative of the victim, sided with the newspapers in a sustained outcry against Scotland Yard. So I sent for the man, my ostensible object being to satisfy him that the Police were doing their duty. As I cross-examined him on the case he gave himself away over and over again. In any French court a report of that interrogation might have convicted the criminal. In an English court it would have raised a storm that might have brought my official career to a close! I never tried that game again.

If I speak of "my reign at Scotland Yard" I may seem to ignore the Chief Commissioner of Police. But it is a popular mistake to suppose that "Scotland Yard" represents the Metropolitan Police. Until the new building on the Embankment was opened the Commissioner's office was in Whitehall Place, whereas the original office of the Detective Department was a building which stood till lately in the middle of Scotland Yard—a place which has fallen from the greatness of other days, when the Scottish kings and their ambassadors lodged there. That the new buildings were christened New Scotland Yard is due to Mr. Monro's love for his old department, for it was in his time as Chief Commissioner that we moved to the Embankment.

I have already noticed the origin of the Criminal Investigation Department in 1878. The only grudge I have against my friend the late General William Feilding[1] is due to my

[1] See p. 125, *ante*.

suspicion that it was he who coined that Frenchified title for the detective department of the Force. Or possibly he shares the blame with Howard Vincent, its first chief. The title is a mouthful, and I will henceforth use the cipher by which it is known in the Force and call it the C.I.D. Vincent was not under the Commissioner of Police, though his subordinates, of course, were members of the Force, and subject to the discipline of the Force; so that he was entirely dependent on the co-operation of the Police generally in his efforts to cope with crime. As I have said before, no one but Howard Vincent could have made such a system work. When he retired, the C.I.D. became an *imperium in imperio*, its chief having the same statutory and disciplinary powers as the other Assistant Commissioners. The outside working of the machine is public property, and may here be explained, for the knowledge may possibly be both interesting and useful to the public. But if any one takes up these pages in expectation of learning the secrets of the department, he may throw them down at once. For I cannot speak too highly of the sense of honour which prevails, not only among the officers, but among the pensioned officers, of the C.I.D. in regard to all matters of which they have official knowledge.

I had a notable proof of this a quarter of a century ago. Political feeling ran high in those days, and rumours which were freely current in society circles seemed to afford material to check the influence of a certain prominent public man. Facts were the desideratum, and money was abundant with those who were in search of evidence. But though liberal offers were made to several pensioned officers who could have given the needed facts, they one after another refused to disclose them, and this because their knowledge was gained in the course of their official duties.

But as to the machine. The Metropolitan Police district extends over a radius of 15 miles from Charing Cross; and it covers an area of 700 square miles, extending from Colney Heath, Hertfordshire, on the north, to Mogadore, Todworth Heath, Surrey, in the south, and from Lark Hall, Essex, on the east, to Staines Moor, Middlesex, in the west. The population of this vast province increases at the rate of some 100,000 a year, and is now about seven and a half millions; more than Canada, with a territory almost as large as Europe, and considerably more than Australia, with an almost equal area. Now any one can appreciate the difference between looking for a person in a country village and in a huge town ; and the problem which daily faces the Chief of the C.I.D. is to find criminals hidden among the seven millions of people who are crowded together in London. Like a spider in the centre of a monster web, he is in touch with every part of the Metropolis ; and every crime committed is immediately reported to him. The system is an adjustment of centralisation with decentralisation. "Unity of design, and responsibility of its agents," was Peel's statement of the main principle on which the Metropolitan Police was organised. The whole Force is a unit ; and yet London is parcelled out in twenty-one divisions, each of which is under its own Superintendent. And to each division is attached an Inspector of the C.I.D., with a staff of officers of the department under him. Police action thus follows on the commission of a crime as promptly as though each division were a separate town, and yet the unity of the whole is maintained. And every officer, though part of this vast machine, acts as though he stood alone.

Sydney Smith it was who said that with him the only illusion left in life was the Archbishop of Canterbury. Like "Cantuar," the office of Constable is of great antiquity. And it is of unique importance. The duties of an officer, as he patrols a London street, may seem almost mechanical in their simplicity. And yet at any moment he may find himself in circumstances fitted to tax his energies and to test his intelligence. And he must act with discretion, and not without some knowledge of the criminal law. Here lies the difference between the soldier and the constable. The soldier's duty is limited to obeying the orders of his officer, and he has no authority beyond what is derived from the orders he receives. But the constable is not only clothed with statutory powers, numerous and far-reaching, but further (as Blackstone tells us), he "hath great original and inherent authority." We all know the story of the children who were discussing the relative importance of the professions of their respective fathers. One of them, the child of the parson, was enlarging on the dignity of the clerical calling when the other, the doctor's child, cut in with the answer, "But my pa could kill your pa." And although the Lord Chancellor or the Prime Minister is a far greater personage than a policeman, yet if one of these great dignitaries should stand at a street corner at night to meditate on his dignity, the policeman on the beat might run him in for "loitering with intent." And no one but a police constable has such power as that.

There is no recorded instance of a First Lord of the Treasury being thus run in; but I remember well a night, some forty years ago, when this happened to a clerk of the department. The story was current when I first came to London that Lord Palmerston, on being asked by an influential supporter for a temporary clerkship in the Treasury for a nominee of his, exclaimed "Impossible! but if you have a friend who wants a bishopric or anything in reason, let me know." My friend was a temporary clerk in the Treasury, and he thought himself "a tremendous swell"; but he was taken to Walton Street Police Station and made to give an account of himself. There was no doubt that he was loitering, though not with felonious intent.

Some one may fancy that it is to "magnify my office" that I have written this. But I myself never enjoyed such powers. I never was a constable, though when I resigned office the Treasury insisted on according me that dignity. But this was merely a pretext to enable them to defraud me in fixing my pension. A Police Commissioner has no powers save those which are expressly conferred on him by the Police Acts, or which pertain to him as a magistrate. For under the Metropolitan Police Acts each of the Commissioners is a magistrate for all the

Home Counties; and he has all the legal powers of a magistrate, though forbidden by statute to act in Sessions. I may add here that when I was appointed I was surprised to find that my colleagues had never taken the oath, for as a lawyer I held this to be essential. Being snubbed for declaring my view of the matter, I naturally pressed it, and the Law Officers, to whom it was referred, supported me. Accordingly we all took the oath as magistrates before the Lord Chancellor.

CHAPTER X

Major Henri Le Caron's life-story—Sir C. Russell's denunciation and Sir H. James's defence of him—A tribute to his high character and his services to the State—Incidents illustrating his work.

THOUGH no one could imagine that Scotland Yard would prove a haven of rest, I did expect to enter on my new duties without disturbance from extraneous causes. But the very month of my appointment the Parnell Special Commission began its sittings, and I was soon dragged into fame over the *affaire Le Caron.*

Irish "Nationalists" would like to erect a statue to any one who displays quixotic zeal for "the cause"; but an Englishman who gives proof of quixotic love for his country they regard with hatred and contempt. They may yet erect a statue in Dublin to Patrick Ford, the dynamiter, while their aim is to brand Henri Le Caron's name with infamy. I cannot prevent their honouring Ford, but I would appeal to

Irish generosity to do justice to Le Caron. Though I had corresponded with the man for twenty years, and he always came to see me when he crossed the Atlantic to visit his people in Colchester, I never really knew him until after his appearance as a witness at the Special Commission. Soon afterwards he contracted a delicacy which ultimately developed into a fatal illness; and this led him to settle in London. During his last years I thus came to know him; and the more I saw of him, and the better I knew him, the higher was the estimate I formed of his character. And I frankly own that till then I never unreservedly accepted his own estimate of his work as being entirely disinterested and patriotic.

He was the son of a Mr. Beach, a worthy and respected citizen of Colchester. A thirst for adventure led him to leave home again and again in early life; and while still a boy he found himself in Paris without either friends or money, or knowledge of the language. But having been a choir-boy in the parish church at home, he attended the English Church in the Rue d'Aguesseau; and his singing secured for him the friendship of a member of the congregation, and led to his obtaining a comfortable berth in the French capital. The outbreak of the American

Civil War in 1861 aroused once more his love of adventure; and crossing the Atlantic he enlisted in the Northern Army. In due course he obtained a commission, and during his service he struck up a friendship with John O'Neill, who afterwards became head of the American Fenians.

Le Caron joined the Fenian conspiracy with the quixotic purpose of thus doing a service to his native country; and in letters to his father he reported all Fenian doings and projects. These letters were shown to Mr. Rebow, M.P. for Colchester, and by him their contents were passed on to the Home Office, no pecuniary reward being either paid or solicited. But after the Clerkenwell explosion Mr. Rebow urged that Le Caron should be put in direct communication with some representative of Government, and I was asked to deal with him. Thus commenced a correspondence which lasted until he decided to give evidence for the *Times* newspaper, twenty years afterwards.

Morley's "Life of Gladstone" avers that "for more than twenty years he was in the pay of Scotland Yard." I have described the Irish section of that work as an "Historical Romance," and the above statement is a fair specimen of the errors that abound in it. "Scotland Yard" was not aware of the man's existence until he appeared as a witness at the Parnell Commission.

At the Special Commission Sir Charles Russell denounced him as a common informer. "His life," he declared, "was a living lie. He wormed himself into the confidence of men presumably honest, however mistaken in their views, only to make money and betray them." This and much more in the same vein drew from Sir Henry James a severe rebuke. "The words of my learned friend," he said, "do not represent the views of a high-minded English gentleman." And he met the attack upon the witness, first by taunting the Parnellite members with taking both the Fenian oath and their oath of allegiance to their Sovereign, and then by describing the aims and methods of the Fenians. The taunt was neither generous nor just. It applied with full force to some of the M.P.s; but they were a small minority. The fact, however, that a few of their colleagues did take both the Fenian oath and the oath of allegiance ought to modify their denunciation of Le Caron.

And his taking the Fenian oath is the one act in Le Caron's service which I regret. To appreciate his work aright some knowledge is needed of the character and aims of the Fenianism of early days. The movement was designed to make Ireland an independent nation, with a republican form of Government. And the American branch of the brotherhood, which was neither oath-bound nor even secret, was organised solely to supply men, arms, and money for the struggle in Ireland. And with some exceptions the leaders on both sides were men of probity and honour. James Stephens was a conceited and unscrupulous impostor, and O'Donovan Rossa was a thoroughly bad man. But the other leaders who were brought to trial at the Special Commission of 1865 were men of whom no Irishman need be ashamed; and the same was true of John O'Mahony, the founder of the American Fenian Brotherhood. John O'Neill's project of raiding Canada was a departure from the original scheme, and a revolt against O'Mahony's leadership. And it was to thwart that scheme that Le Caron joined the brotherhood "as a military spy in the service of his country."

I presume that in the judgment of a doctrinaire republican the Fenianism of the sixties would be deemed a legitimate political agitation. But when the blunders and frauds of dishonest and incompetent men brought discredit on the movement, and proved its projects to be impracticable, men of the type of Patrick Ford of the *Irish World* newspaper came to the front, and American Fenianism became a secret society for the promotion of fiendish crime. The change reached a crisis in 1875 when Ford established the "skirmishing fund," of which more anon. The Fenian raid on Canada, which was turned into a fiasco by Le Caron's services, occurred in 1870. During the intervening years, though he was not "in the pay of the British Government," his correspondence with me never flagged, and his letters contained much valuable information by which our Government profited. But when the change above indicated occurred in American Fenianism he responded to the appeal I made to him to help us in this new danger. And I maintain emphatically that all he did was on the lines of ordinary Police duty in dealing with criminals and crime—a fact which was not ignored in Sir Henry James's defence of him.

The wife of an acquaintance of mine, a well-known man whose death occurred a few months ago, was roused one night by a noise downstairs. On entering the dining-room she was confronted by a burglar who at once struck her a violent blow. Instead of screaming for assistance she began to appeal to him on the plane of benevolence and Christian duty. The man put down the booty he had collected; but he declared that he must have money : Where would he find money? She told him she had only £5 in the house, and this she gave him and let him go. Not many months elapsed before that money was returned to her by post. I do not envy those who would sneer at this simple narrative of facts. And sure I am that no one will suffer by acting, in his private capacity, on these transcendental principles. But if it be a question of our *duty*, we must remember that in this matter duty is limited to speaking the truth *to our neighbour;* and a burglar is not our neighbour. He is an outlaw ; and instead of telling him where to find our money, we hand him over to the constable on the beat. And the duty of the constable is not to play the philanthropist, but to bring the criminal to justice.

The better sort of Police official finds pleasure in befriending men who have been thus brought to justice, and helping them upon their way; for some of them are worthy of help. But the assassins and dynamiters whose plots were exposed by Le Caron were justly described by Sir Henry James as "enemies of the human race, the lowest and most degraded of beings, unfit to be regarded as belonging to the human community." Are such men, he indignantly demanded, to be regarded as "presumably honest?" He justly claimed that Le Caron and his work should be viewed in the light in which detective Police work is regarded. Not only so, but, as he went on to say, "the community praise the exertions of a man who apprehends the criminal after the crime has been committed. But here you have a man who, running risks such as probably no one ever ran before, set himself to defeat crime before it was carried out, and thus to save the lives of those who had no other protection." In this sense, and in this sense alone, it was that Le Caron betrayed the Fenians; for in not a single instance was a criminal charge ever brought against any one upon his testimony, either in this country or in America.

But, we are told, he betrayed them for the sake of gain. This is a base slander. As a matter of fact the man was singularly indifferent to money. Though his letters to me never ceased, and the information they brought was always useful, there were several years during which no money grant whatever was made to him. The only really important payment he ever received was his reward for thwarting the 1870 Fenian raid on Canada; and when I wrote to apprise him of the grant, he replied that his wife begged I would keep the money for him, and dole it out to him as and when he wanted it. And as a matter of fact I kept back half the amount in this way. At every Fenian convention that he attended as a delegate, he was entitled to receive his expenses from the organisation—and the Fenians never studied economy in their claims upon the war chest—but he would not touch Fenian money.

His professional income as a medical practitioner enabled him to maintain this independent position. And this it was that gave him such influence with the Fenians, and enabled him to be so useful as an informant. It emboldened him, for instance, to send me the secret documents issued by the organisation. For as "Senior Guardian of a Camp," or, in other words, chief officer of a Fenian Lodge, he received a copy of every document of the kind. But though our Consuls in New York and Chicago, &c., had agents holding office in the brotherhood, no one of them ever dared to part with such documents. For he was liable at any time to be called upon to produce them, and his failure to do so would have cost him his life. And considering the number of years that Le Caron thus put his life in my hands, it is a marvel that he escaped. I need not say that I used the utmost care, and always returned his papers promptly; but even the most careful among us may be caught napping at times. And the risk of a slip was increased by the fact that our correspondence was carried on through his wife on that side, and a lady relative of mine on this; for his name and mine were too well known to make direct communication safe.

These precautions, I may say, were not of his devising, for he was as indifferent to danger as to money. And as for the money, when I first met him in 1869, and arranged details for our correspondence, it was I, not he, who raised the question of remuneration. His rôle, as he said from the first, was that of "a military spy in the service of his country." Till then he had corresponded on Fenian matters with no one but his own father, and he emphatically refused to deal with "a Government office." But I gave him the promise, which I always faithfully kept, that his letters to me would be treated precisely as his letters to his father had been treated; that I would regard them as private, while communicating to Government the information they contained.

On two occasions I asked him to relieve me of this promise. The first was when Colonel Brackenbury became Assistant Under-Secretary for Police and Crime in Ireland. And when his successor went to Dublin Castle I wrote again to Le Caron that if he would yield the point he would be certain of liberal remuneration—remuneration on a far higher scale than he had ever received in the past. But this letter brought me such a petulantly indignant reply that I never raised the question again.

My first Fenian informant was shot like a dog on returning to New York. In communicating the man's information to Lord Mayo, then Chief Secretary, I gave him the poor fellow's name, and some particulars respecting him, and these he passed on to the Lord-Lieutenant as they sat together one evening over the dinner-table at the Viceregal Lodge. A servant happened to be behind the screen which covered the service door of the dining-room, and he overheard the conversation, and repeated it in the servants' hall. This I learned from the detective Superintendent of Police at Dublin Castle; and in telling me the facts he added the warning—being himself an old hand at that sort of work—never to trust any one with the name of an informant. I profited by his advice, and from that day no informant of mine was ever betrayed. I suppose there are people upon whom the responsibility would weigh lightly of having a man's life in their hands. But I am "not made that way." This it was, quite as much as my sense of the thankless character of the work—of which I have lately had such signal proof—that made me try again and again to escape from Secret Service duties.

In his "Twenty-five Years in the Secret Service,"[1] Le Caron mentions two incidents which illustrate the risks he ran in his work. Of the one I will say nothing here: it was a dastardly business. But the other has an amusing side to it. When in the spring of 1870 John O'Neill, the President of the American Fenian organisation, was preparing for his raid on Canada, I felt that it was essential to put Le Caron in communication with some representative of the Dominion Government, and Judge M'Micken undertook this delicate part. He was the only person on that side of the Atlantic who knew of Le Caron's work for me. This is chapter one of my story. Chapter two is that when Sir William Harcourt took up Secret Service work, he asked Sir John Rose, who was then about to cross the Atlantic, to make inquiries with a view to strengthening our anti-Fenian organisation; and on his return to London, Sir William summoned me to 7, Grafton Street to meet him. Sir John Rose told us that Judge M'Micken had named Major Le Caron to him as a man who, if we could enlist his services, would be a most valuable ally to Government.

[1] Pp. 272, 273.

But of course the Judge did not disclose the fact that he had given help of the kind in the past. Sir John Rose went on to say that his inquiries in New York fully bore out M'Micken's estimate of the man. Then Sir William Harcourt turned to me and asked me if I knew him. I replied that I knew him well, and I gave them many facts respecting him. The next question was whether the man would assist our Government; and my answer to that was that a proposal to such a man to give information to the Police or a Government office would be regarded as an insult. The right course, I said, would be to refer the matter to Judge M'Micken. Here is the account of the result, which Le Caron gives in his book: "So strong was the pressure put upon the Judge that he travelled specially to Chicago to see me on the point. However" (he adds) "I would have none of it." If Le Caron had yielded to the overtures then made to him he might have named his own terms.

One more incident, selected to illustrate the need for unceasing care lest in using information one should betray the informant. On leaving the House of Commons on the night of the 23rd of May, 1881, Le Caron drove to my house, and reported to me in full detail his historic interview with Parnell. And in doing so he cynically remarked, "Now, if you want to get rid of me, here is your chance!" meaning that to repeat his story would get him a bullet on his return to New York. What was I to do? For to suppress information of such importance was out of the question. I escaped by keeping back my report till I received a letter from him after he reached home; and then I gave the whole story as "received from an American informant."

During the four-and-thirty years of my official life I came to entertain a sincere regard for not a few of the Police officers who assisted me in my campaigns against criminals, but none of them did I esteem more highly than Le Caron. And it is with them that I have always classed him, and not with secret agents and informants. No bad man could win, as he won, the unbounded respect of wife and children. To his good qualities, moreover, were added many characteristics which made him attractive and popular. And to his personal charm he added sterling integrity. He was one of the most truthfully accurate men I have ever known. Even men holding high office may indulge in "terminological inexactitudes," and very few people are capable of repeating accurately a conversation of yesterday; but I never detected Le Caron in a serious inaccuracy. Nor had I ever to complain of either concealment or exaggeration in his communications to me. So much for Henri Le Caron. Though he deserves well of his country, he will never get a statue. But if he is to be pilloried I will take my place by his side.

CHAPTER XI

The dynamiters and their work — Patrick Ford's "Skirmishing Fund"—The Irish National League Convention, 1881—The Convention of 1886—The Queen's Jubilee plot—The dynamite plot of 1896; the case of Ivory *alias* Bell—Home Office consultations—An interview with Lord Salisbury—Luncheon at Walmer—Quixotic action of the law officers—Changed relations between Great Britain and the United States—Amnesty of Fenian convicts in 1869 —Rescue plots—Plot to murder Mr. Chamberlain—The Transvaal Raid—Proceedings at Bow Street against Dr. Jameson, &c.—Criticism of our methods of taking evidence.

SIR HENRY JAMES'S estimate of the dynamiters and their work was just. Indeed, no language could be too strong to characterise such miscreants and to denounce their projects. And people need to be reminded of these things, for a new generation has grown up that knows nothing of them. In 1877 the Fenian Skirmishing Fund, established two years before by Patrick Ford of the *Irish World* newspaper, was transferred to a Committee with O'Donovan

Rossa as Secretary. But Rossa was accused of embezzling the money and was soon shelved. In 1881 a charge of the same kind was brought against Ford himself; and in his defence he unblushingly published the history of the fund in his newspaper, giving the names of the trustees, and declaring that they held the money in trust "to lay the big cities of England in ashes." And Ford's was the first signature to the public circular summoning the Irish National Convention of that year, at which some of Mr. Parnell's principal lieutenants were present. The proceedings of that Convention were open, and they were reported in Irish-American newspapers. But, as the Fenian leader John Devoy imprudently disclosed in *The Irish Nation*, "the number of conferences and caucuses held in the intervals between the sessions of the Convention was almost without number, and it was here the real work was done," the real work being to further the dynamite campaign.

In other words, the public convention was merely a screen behind which the Fenian outrage-mongers settled their plans. "Our policy," they declared in a secret circular issued to the Fenian lodges, "will be to make assaults in all directions, so that the suffering, bitterness, and desolation which follow active measures shall be felt in every place." And the dynamite outrages in this country during succeeding years were the outcome of those meetings. I may here record that thirty-two of the dynamite emissaries were brought to justice, and seventeen of them received life sentences.

The scheme of using the annual Irish National Convention to further the Fenian outrage campaign succeeded so well in 1881 that it was followed in subsequent years, and with very practical results in 1883 and 1886. The public meetings of the 1886 Convention, which were attended as usual by some of the Parnellite M.P.'s, ended on August 19th; and on the following day the Fenian caucus met and issued a circular announcing the early renewal of active operations; "a pyrotechnic display in honour of Queen Victoria's Jubilee" being specially indicated. The main particulars of that hellish plot have been already given, and I need not repeat them here. And if I speak of the last dynamite plot of ten years later I do so, not only because it is noteworthy as being the last of the series, but also because it illustrates the quixotic principles on which we deal with outlaws charged with these fiendish crimes. It is connected, moreover, with an interesting episode in the course of my official work.

Ivory, *alias* Bell, was the leader of a gang of dynamiters who crossed the Atlantic in August, 1896. He landed at Antwerp and made his way from there to Glasgow, where he was arrested on September 12th. His chief confederate, Tynan by name—the No. 1 of the Phœnix Park murder plot—came to Boulogne, and the others found what they supposed to be a safe retreat at Rotterdam. But they were all arrested by the local police, and they were held in custody until the collapse of the case against Ivory. And the cause of that collapse is the point of my story. The gentleman who deserves the credit of exposing the plot profited, of course, by information received from one of the party, a man who had gone as far as was safe for him to do in checking the schemes of his confederates. When I reported the case to the Secretary of State, the fact that one of the gang had given information seemed to him to be a bar to a Government prosecution. I urged that if such a view were to prevail, all Police action in dealing with organised crime would be paralysed; and as the case involved a demand for the extradition of the men in custody at Rotterdam and Boulogne, Sir Matthew Ridley decided to lay the matter before Lord Salisbury, and he directed me to accompany him.

Next morning we travelled down to Walmer, the Prime Minister being then at the Castle surrounded by his family circle. The Home Secretary laid the facts of the case before him, explaining the view he had formed. But he added, "Anderson differs from me entirely, and I will ask you to hear what he has to say about it." Neither while Sir Matthew Ridley was speaking, nor when I took up my parable, did Lord Salisbury indicate in any way what was working in his mind; but, "the arguments concluded," he asked a number of questions, and then gave his decision, adopting unreservedly the view I had been pressing.

As I am dealing with the lighter side of official matters I pause here, for at that moment the luncheon bell sounded, and Lord Salisbury rose and led us to the dining-room. No one else had yet come in, and as he sat down at the head of the table without indicating any particular place for me, my native modesty led me to take what I supposed to be "the lowest room." But when the house party gathered, the Marchioness took her place at that end of the table, and then the Marquis rose and came to sit by me on the other side. It was quite a new reading of the parable!

The conversation during luncheon was full of

interest. Among other matters, the French *conseil de famille* system was explained and extolled. In a recent case here a man who had inherited a fortune squandered it by gambling and dissipation, thus reducing his family to poverty, and Lord Salisbury explained the provisions of the French code for preventing disasters of that kind. The Channel Tunnel scheme also came up for discussion; and speaking, as he said pointedly, only as a traveller, Lord Salisbury expressed a strong desire that the project might be realised. When I remarked that I often crossed the Channel for pleasure, the look he gave me, and the tone in which he repeated the words "for pleasure," made me glad I had already said my say on the dynamite case!

After luncheon Lord Salisbury brought me out to the terrace and kept me talking with him until Sir Matthew Ridley came to summon me to catch the four o'clock train to town. At table I had been a greatly interested listener, my part in the conversation being confined almost entirely to asking questions; and on the terrace I tried to keep to the same *rôle*. But when two wills conflict, the weaker always gives way, and during the hour we sat there the Prime Minister turned the tables on me, making me talk on various subjects, including, of course, Ireland and the Irish.

Another pleasant memory of that trip to Walmer was the generous assurance I received from the Secretary of State on our journey back to town that he was greatly gratified at my having satisfied the Prime Minister that the Ivory case might be allowed to proceed. And on the official file he afterwards expressed his "full approval" of all the action taken by the Police. But it was not to be. The man was brought to trial before Mr. Justice Hawkins at the January, 1897, sessions of the Central Criminal Court, and on the second day (January 19th) I was summoned to another conference at the Home Office. I found the Law Officers in the Secretary of State's room, and I learned that, on hearing that one of the gang had given information, they had decided to withdraw from the prosecution. When the Judge took his seat on the bench next morning Ivory stood forward with a paper in his hand to address the Court, but the Solicitor-General interposed to announce the decision at which the Law Officers had arrived.

And now for my side of the story. The gentleman entrusted with the defence of Ivory had warned me months before that he was aware of the source of our knowledge of the plot, and that if the case proceeded he would expose the whole business as the work of an *agent provocateur*. My answer was that, while the credit of detecting the plot was not mine, I unreservedly accepted responsibility for everything that had been done; and I advised him to consult his client before attempting that line of defence. On the very day of our last Home Office conference he called again to say, in strict confidence, that Ivory would withdraw his plea of not guilty if I would undertake to get him a light sentence. But he trusted to my honour not to inform either the Home Secretary or the Law Officers of his visit to me. I told him, of course, that on those conditions I could give no pledge of the kind. But I added that my relations not only with the Home Secretary and the Attorney- and Solicitor-General, but also with the presiding Judge, were of such a character that I felt confident that if the prisoner would openly express regret for his share in the dynamite conspiracy I could obtain an early remission of his sentence. The Solicitor-General's intervention prevented the accused from making a statement in this sense on the third day of the trial.

Such are our ways with dynamiters. These

men were not Britishers, but aliens who came over in time of peace to perpetrate outrages, which if committed by soldiers in time of war, would ensure them short shrift after trial by drumhead court-martial. And, as proved by the experience of the crimes which were brought to maturity, their victims were invariably people who took no part in our political life. And yet these miscreants were treated with a quixotic leniency that would not be extended to ordinary criminals. For the measures adopted to detect *quasi* political crime in no way differ from those by which every competent Police Force deals with organised crime of any kind. If the informant be the one who directs or finances the crime, he may reasonably be suspected of playing the *agent provocateur;* but no suspicion of that kind ever rests on one of the rank and file. And while every man who takes part in ordinary crime does so freely and deliberately, these secret societies have ways of putting pressure on a member to join in acts which may not be to his liking.

And any highly trained Police ought to be able to thwart organised crime, whether the project be treasonable or fraudulent. But to catch a criminal who works alone and keeps his own counsel is a far higher test of skill. And in the case of dynamiters, it may also be a severe test of nerves. I never spent hours of greater anxiety than during one afternoon in February, 1894, when information reached me that a French tailor named Bourdin had left his shop in Soho with a bomb in his pocket. To track him was impracticable. All that could be done was to send out officers in every direction to watch persons and places that he might be likely to attack. His actual objective was the very last place the Police would have thought of watching, namely Greenwich Observatory. Travelling to Greenwich by tramcar, he entered the Park, and as he ascended the path leading to the Observatory he evidently took the bomb out of his pocket, and was preparing to use it, when it exploded in his hand, inflicting injuries from which he died after a few hours' suffering.

This case further illustrates what I have said about dynamiters and their crimes. In war the guns of an enemy would no doubt spare an astronomical Observatory, for none but savages would wish to injure an institution of that kind ; but these fiends are the enemies of humanity. And this Bourdin was an alien anarchist who was living here only by the courtesy of our law, or, I should be rather disposed to say, by the criminal apathy with which our law is administered. For the anarchist conspiracy is treasonable, and every one who even takes part in a Soho meeting in furtherance of its projects might be criminally charged—a fact that was ignored by the British delegates to the anti-anarchist convention held in Rome in 1898.

My mentioning that the Fenian dynamiters were aliens reminds me of the marked and happy change which has taken place in our relations with the Government and people of the United States.

When I came to Whitehall forty-three years ago the Secretary to the American Embassy in London—and he was a man of much influence at the Embassy—was an Anglophobe. And the Washington dispatches of that era contained many a stern and petulant remonstrance against the imprisonment of the American citizens who had taken an active part in the Fenian conspiracy in Ireland. Facts, moreover, seemed to give proof that there was some truth in the blatant boast of the American-Irish of that day, that the attitude of the U.S. Government toward Fenianism was one of benevolent neutrality. This was due in part, no doubt, to the influence of the Irish vote; but the Irish vote would not have sufficed had it not been for the distrust and dislike of England which very generally prevailed in political circles. It was the fear of America that ensured "equal justice" for aliens and for

British subjects who were convicted of treason or treason felony; and "equal justice" is often flagrantly unjust. If the aliens had been hanged, and the British subjects had been treated with greater leniency, it would have done more to suppress Fenianism; but it would have raised a tremendous storm in America.

I always pitied the Irish Fenian convicts of 1865 and 1867. The journalists who were sent to penal servitude in the former year deserved a better fate, and the men who took part in the "Fenian rising" of 1867 were hardly dealt with. And no one now living has a better knowledge of the facts; for when the prisoners of the "rising" in Co. Dublin—they were numbered by hundreds—were committed for trial, the Attorney-General entrusted to me the task of looking into all their cases, and advising him as to their relative degrees of guilt.

Judging, as they naturally do, by the ways of Irishmen who are prominent in political life, English people have come to form a very unfavourable estimate of our national characteristics. But the better sort of Irishman does not hate and slander every one who differs from him. On the contrary, he is glad to help a fellow-countryman. And to me it was that the Fenian convicts released in 1869 were indebted for being allowed to eat their Christmas dinner as free men. The question of granting such an amnesty had been for some time under discussion between Downing Street, Whitehall, and Dublin Castle, but it was not till the advent of Christmas that a final decision was arrived at ; and then it was that the sentiment of Christmas found vent in the matter. Mr. Gladstone expressed an earnest wish that their discharge should take place on Christmas Eve. This, however, was declared to be impossible, as it involved the preparation of a huge sheaf of warrants, each one of which had to be signed by the Queen.

I was with the Secretary of State when this was communicated to him, and at the same time the Premier's private secretary came in to express Mr. Gladstone's disappointment and distress. I turned to Mr. Bruce and offered the opinion that there was no difficulty whatever in the matter ; a single warrant would suffice, with a schedule giving the names of the convicts to whom it referred. A reference to "The Office" elicited that such a proceeding was "impracticable," and a hurried reference to the Law Officers resulted in their expressing a doubt whether it would be legal. This led me to remind Mr. Bruce that all the cases involved were Irish, and I obtained his leave to lay the matter before the Irish Law

Officers, who happened to be then in London. After a brief conference in the law-room of the Irish Office, I returned with their decision in favour of my view. The warrant was prepared, a special messenger carried it to Windsor, and the convicts were released next day.

Cases of special gravity were not included in that amnesty, and when the Patrick Ford gang inaugurated their outrage campaign, one of their projects was a forcible rescue of the Fenian convicts still remaining in custody. And this presently gave place to the still wilder scheme of kidnapping some prominent public man—by preference the Prince of Wales or the Prime Minister! and holding him as a hostage for their release. This plot seemed so absurd that, although tidings of it reached me from a trustworthy source, I was disposed to scout it. But information to the same effect was received in Dublin Castle, with the additional detail that money to give effect to it had come from Ford's Skirmishing Fund; and the Irish Government considered that it ought not to be ignored. Such plots, I may remark, were not infrequently announced as an excuse for embezzling that fund, and I daresay the plot in question was in that category; but nothing occurred on which to base a decision. For if any serious plot of the kind really existed, it was thwarted by the police precautions adopted at the time. And it is unnecessary to add that an attempt to give practical effect to it would have meant murder.

Murder plots were common with these criminals. That which culminated in the Phœnix Park tragedy is known to everybody, but the public know nothing of many similar plots that were thwarted by Police action. When Mr. Chamberlain visited America in 1896 there was a formidable plot to assassinate him at the home where he was sojourning in Pennsylvania. Facts which came to light convinced the local Police of the truth of the information received, and the American authorities deemed it necessary to take very special measures for his protection.

Yet another case of historic interest occurred in 1896. In February of that year Dr. Jameson and the other leaders in the Transvaal Raid of the closing days of 1895 were arrested and charged at Bow Street. Several of the troopers who took part in the Raid were brought to England by the Treasury to give information and evidence in the case. And the gossip of these men disclosed an incident connected with the Raid which escaped notice at the time. They declared that as they were marching straight for Johannesburg, with nothing to stop them, a stranger, who proved to be an emissary of wily old Kruger, appeared in the camp, coming from nobody knew where, and ingratiated himself with the military leaders of the expedition. He expressed great delight on learning the object of their march. But, he told them, they were on the wrong road, and he knew every inch of the country. Their trustworthy guide, in spite of his assurances and protests, was sent to the rear in disgrace; and, led by Kruger's spy, the column was marched into the Boer ambuscade which brought the expedition to an end.

That case is associated in my mind with a question of much practical importance respecting the procedure in our criminal courts. The head of the C.I.D. seldom attends a police-court, but the historic interest and the importance of the Jameson Raid led me to go to Bow Street when the accused were brought up. But a few hours of it were as much as I could stand. The intolerable tediousness of the mode in which the evidence was taken was worthy of the Dark Ages. Counsel asked a question, and the witness replied. The Chief Magistrate and the lawyers sat waiting while, with great deliberation, the Clerk of the Court wrote down the answer, and read out what he had written. And then, provided no dispute arose as to the accuracy of the record, the next question was put to the witness. The odd shillings of the guineas marked on the briefs of the distinguished lawyers in the case would have paid the cost of employing several shorthand reporters, and the work of that afternoon might have been far better done in a single hour. For our present methods do not even ensure accuracy; and of course a real cross-examination is often thwarted.

This reminds me of another *bétise* that marks our proceedings in criminal courts. I refer to requiring that a witness, when repeating the statement of other persons, shall give their *ipsissima verba*, and in the first person. There is an old Bar story of a judge who cut in when counsel failed to get a truthful witness to "toe the line" in this way. "Witness," the Judge asked, "did the prisoner say 'I stole the horse'?" "Oh, no, my lord," the man replied in a deprecatory tone, "your lordship's name was never mentioned."

I once had an experience of giving evidence on this system myself. At a dinner party at one of the historic houses of London many years ago, the conversation turned upon curries, and it was remarked that very few English cooks knew how to boil rice. I said that my cook excelled in that respect. "Keep her, drunk or sober!" exclaimed an old gentleman sitting near me. I did, and with evil consequences! She had a follower, and, incited by an old thief of his acquaintance, he made the woman drunk one night, and together the two men raided the house. I was away with my family on my summer holiday when a telegram, announcing that "burglars had broken in," brought me back to town. As this was the fourth year that the woman had been left in charge of my house, I had no suspicions whatever of her honesty, and I talked with her freely about the felony. But the Police knew better, and they arrested her along with the actual thieves. Thus it came about that, some weeks after the event, I was called upon to give evidence against her. I felt perfectly competent to give the substance of all she had said to me, but I jibbed when called on to repeat in detail, and on oath, the exact words she used in the various conversations I had held with her. Though there is not one man in ten thousand who could do this truthfully after the lapse of several weeks, it was required of me, as it is required of every witness. It was with great qualms of conscience that I yielded. And when the case came on at the Central Criminal

Court, I escaped discredit only by carefully reading up the report of what I had said before the Magistrate.

The system is as stupid as it is evil, and it tends to defeat justice. In the year of the Jameson Raid I succeeded in getting a good case against an infamous couple who had long been engaged in "the white slave traffic"; but they escaped because their victim, a Belgian girl, could not be induced to commit this modified sort of perjury. As the Magistrate knew no French, the conduct of the case was practically left to the Clerk of the Court, a man whose knowledge of the language was not so great as his conceit, and he persuaded the Bench that the witness, a thoroughly respectable and truthful young woman, was unreliable because she adhered to a statement of the facts and *the gist* of her conversations with the accused.

CHAPTER XII

Work at Scotland Yard—The exacting demands of police duty—Antiquated methods—Red tape—Home Office ways: Liddell and Lushington contrasted—An incident of 1893—The Liberals and Home Rule—Sir John Gray on Irish grievances—An Irish story—Arrest of two Irish M.P.'s in 1891, and a night at Scotland Yard—The new journalism, and Press "interviews"—Jabez Balfour's case—A Strand explosion.

A CYNIC might ask what the heavy side of my official life was like, if these pages represent its lighter side. Well, I suppose I am like the old lady's parrot that did so much thinking that it constantly lapsed into seriousness. But I must try to mend my ways. And yet I do not wish to convey the very false impression that amusement is the prevailing element in Police work. Both my predecessors in office suffered from the strain, and retired after five years of it. And if I was able to bear it for thirteen years, and to be "fitter" on leaving Scotland Yard than when I entered on the duties of the office, this was due mainly to a native sense of humour and an acquired capacity for turning away from anxious and engrossing work. To be able to find amusement in events of grave import is a useful relief to the mind; but to have interests that are infinitely higher and more absorbing than sublunary matters of any kind—this, to put it on the lowest ground, is a mental tonic of inestimable value.

When the ordinary Civil Servant leaves his office in the afternoon, he has a complete respite from Government work for some seventeen hours; and when Saturday comes round, his recess extends to more than forty hours. But Police work in London knows no such leisure. And of the two main branches of Police duty —Public Order and Crime, the latter is, of course, the more exacting. In a very real sense indeed the head of the C.I.D. is never off duty. Every crime committed in this seven-million peopled "province of brick" is reported to him; and all cases of special urgency or importance are reported immediately, day or night. And in my time our methods were somewhat antiquated.

When I first came to London, intercommunication between the various Government offices was conducted on the same system as in the days of Queen Anne. The telephone was a dream of the future, and the offices were not even connected by telegraph. And before I moved from the Irish Office to Whitehall I had two messengers in attendance on me, to carry letters and papers to and from the Home Office. This was in 1868. Soon after I went to Scotland Yard, twenty years later, the telephone was brought into use between our offices and Whitehall; and when we moved to the Embankment it was introduced within the new building. But the houses of the Commissioners were dependent on the telegraph, and we had not yet attained to self-recording instruments. Every message, therefore, had to be spelled out letter by letter. The telegraph, though of course a necessity, was thus a thorough nuisance; and for some occult reason I had more calls during my first year of office than at any subsequent period.

The "red tape" element in Government work is exasperating to any one who has a soul above trivialities. If one of my officers took a 'bus to Oxford Circus or the City, he could not recover the fare without a certificate under my hand. Matters of vastly greater importance were left to the discretion of a Superintendent;

and a minute bearing my initials was sufficient authority for the arrest of a burglar or a murderer. But here I had to give my signature in full on three separate forms, certifying that the charge was legitimate and the amount correct. How my predecessors tolerated such a system is a mystery to me; but before many weeks passed I "went on strike" respecting this and similar imbecilities. I directed the Superintendents to deal with all such matters, and I announced that I would add my initials to one form, and only to one, in each case, and this without examination of the details. Sir Charles Warren was indignant. For he had to sign all the forms in full. "Yes," I said, "and that is further proof of the absurdity of the system, for the Treasury requires your certificate as Chief Commissioner, but mine is only for the Receiver of Police." That settled the matter, for not only was Sir Charles eminently sensible, but he delighted in thwarting the Receiver! This matter may seem too trifling for notice here, but my object is to let the public see behind the screen of a Government office, so far as it is in the public interest to do so. Some people believe that if the country were administered by Government offices the millennium would follow: I confidently predict that the resulting millennium would not last a thousand years!

Though a well-oiled wheel does not suffer by being kept turning, a little grit will impair its usefulness. And with a hale man it is not work, but worry, that kills. The work told on Howard Vincent. And yet I often looked back with envy to his days at Scotland Yard. Scores of times have I been in the Under-Secretary's room at the Home Office when he came in to talk about some case of special interest or difficulty. But instead of Liddell, I had to do with Lushington. Now Liddell, though he never played tennis with me, or dined at my table, would always have been ready to give sympathetic advice and help; but Lushington was a man of a different kidney. By instinct and training he was a doctrinaire Radical, and that means a good deal. I am not speaking as a party politician—for I am not, and have never been, a party man—but as a student of human nature. For my experience of men—which is not a narrow one—satisfies me that the new idea of liberty which prevails in that school is that of the Irish peasant who emigrated to New York. Said he, in a letter to his people at home, "This is a real free country; every one does exactly what he likes, and if he doesn't, begorra, we *make* him do it."

But, whatever the reason, Lushington never gave me any help in my official work ; and when Mr. Monro left Scotland Yard I was thrown on my own resources to an extent unknown by my predecessors in the office. Naturally I made some grave mistakes. But no man is fit to be head of the C.I.D. if he is not clever enough to make mistakes without being caught! And I can boast that I never incurred a word of censure for a single one of my errors; and in one instance—it was matter that cost me much distress and some searchings of heart, for it related to the safety of the Queen—I had a letter of thanks from the Home Office!

Though I was never detected when in the wrong, I was occasionally censured when in the right. Indeed, my relations with the Home Office in those days remind me of Sir William Harcourt's defence of the system on which titles and decorations are granted. "Some people," said he, "get them who don't deserve them, and some people deserve them who don't get them ; and so, on the whole, justice is done!" My old Home Office friend "the Admiral" often gave me good advice, and one of his maxims was useful. "In official life," he said, "never defend yourself. If you are in the wrong, the less you say the better; and if you are in the right, do like the pious coster when his moke kicked him: instead of swearing, he was only sorry the poor creature knew no better!"

The newspapers sometimes got me into trouble in this way. A case of the kind occurred in 1893. It fell upon a day that one of the London newspapers published a lecture supposed to have been delivered by me on Irish Home Rule, which was then a burning political question. Even an habitual criminal if charged with an offence is given a fair hearing before he is condemned; but without asking me for any explanation the Secretary of State fulminated a severe censure upon me. The facts were not disclosed, for I acted on "the Admiral's" advice; but they exemplify the terror that the new journalism has added to official life. A Literary Society connected with the Church of which I am a member had invited me to lecture on Grattan's Irish Parliament. When the evening arrived a tropical rain-storm killed the meeting, and instead of a full lecture-hall I found about a score of people. This was really a relief to me, for pressure of work had prevented my preparing a lecture, and I put them off with a *rechauffé* of my friend Swift MacNeill's valuable book on the subject. After the lecture some half-dozen of us had a conversation in the vestry about Mr. Gladstone's Home Rule scheme ; and in the exercise of my undoubted right as a freeborn Britisher I freely expressed my opinion of that measure. But one of our number, then known to me only as a member of the congregation, happened to be a journalist ; and by his skilful pen the lecture and conversation were woven into a coherent whole, and the result appeared next day in prominent type in the paper with which he was connected.

In those days the Liberals were very touchy about Home Rule. And with good reason. For whatever his admirers may say about Mr. Gladstone's change of front on that question, the sudden conversion of the mass of his followers was scarcely honest. There were individuals among them, no doubt, who had been wavering, and were ready at once to follow the lead he gave them ; but for a whole political party to turn right-about-face in such a matter at a day's notice—this was an event which has lowered the tone of public life in this country. And their leader offered them no bridge by which to cross from one side to the other. With incomparable ability and force he had exposed the falseness of the Home Rule agitation and the evils which its success would entail, and he never made any attempt to refute the powerful arguments he had used in warning the country against it. As a matter of fact, indeed, the narrative of Morley's "Life of Gladstone" gives proof that to the last the Liberal leader was unable to devise any safeguards against the dangers in which Irish Home Rule would involve this country.

A friend of mine tells a characteristic story of one of the pioneers of the Home Rule movement, who was a close personal friend of his. Unlike most of the present Home Rulers, Sir John Gray was a man of substance and influence in Dublin. He owned a leading newspaper, and he it was who promoted and carried the scheme which has given the Irish capital an abundant supply of water. At dinner at my friend's house one evening he was declaiming against the system by which an Irish measure of that kind cannot be carried through without an appeal to Westminster. But "gas and water Home Rule" would not satisfy them. "What would satisfy you?" my friend demanded. Gray evaded the question again and again; but as my friend insisted on an answer, the Home Ruler at last replied with a smile, and a twinkle in his eye, "We don't want to be satisfied!" Here is the naked truth.

An Irish story never comes amiss. After soldiering about the world, the gentleman to whom it relates left the army on his father's death, and came to settle on the Irish family property. He had married a rich wife, and he could afford to make his home comfortable. Some of the old servants were a difficulty, for to dismiss people who had been born and bred on the place was not to be thought of. The coachman was the most troublesome. The horses, he declared, were screws, the carriages were worn out, the stable wasn't fit for a cow-house, his cottage was only fit for pigs, and so on. But everything, he was told, would be put right, including a new cottage for himself. The man went home and delighted his wife's heart with the news. But after supper, as he sat by the fire, with his pipe in his month, he began growling and grumbling. "Well, whatever's wrong wid ye now?" said the wife. "I'm a miserable man this night," he muttered; "begorra, I haven't a single graivance left." The moral of my story will be understood by any one who will read Mr. Swift MacNeill's "Irish Parliament," or even the extracts from it given in my book "A Great Conspiracy." The grant of Gladstonian

Home Rule to Ireland would soon lead to an agitation more vehement and dangerous than any which the present generation has experienced.

But here I am lapsing into the serious vein again, and I must make amends for it by recalling an occasion when I came into touch with two real Home Rulers. On the 12th of February, 1891, the Irish M.P.'s Mr. John Dillon and Mr. William O'Brien returned from France to answer a charge of political crime in Ireland. I sent officers to Boulogne to arrest them on the Channel boat. But what was I to do with them on their arrival? Precedent and duty required that they should either be sent on to Ireland that night, or locked up in the cells of a police station. But I hold very decided views about the treatment of respectable folk on arrest. So, while the prisoners were crossing the Channel, I went to the House of Commons to see the Home Secretary on the matter. I found him in Mr. W. H. Smith's room, and with them Mr. Arthur Balfour, then Chief Secretary. And as the result of my visit I was given a free hand to act in my discretion; but I was to deal with the case as a matter of Police, and without reference to the Secretary of State.

When the prisoners arrived, I found that they objected strongly to doing any more travelling that night. So I told them that if they would accept my hospitality I should try to make them comfortable at Scotland Yard. Mr. O'Brien's response was a peremptory demand to be conveyed to a good hotel. My rejoinder, as I left the room, was a reference to the police cells at King Street. But Mr. Dillon followed me out to the corridor and, begging me "not to mind *him*," expressed his appreciation of my proposal. So there and then I gave the necessary orders, and went back to my own room. Two requests followed me. The first was for permission to see their friends. This was somewhat embarrassing, but I directed that any M.P. might be admitted. The second request, which reached me just as I was leaving for home, is the point of my story. "Might they have a bottle of Irish whisky?" "Certainly," said I; and then, remembering my order about admitting M.P.'s, I added, "Let them have *two* bottles." I have often shown my antipathy to Irish Home Rule; but this was the only opportunity I had of befriending Irish Home Rulers.

It is within living memory that the new journalism has been acclimatised in this country. We all know the child's game in which one of the party is put outside the door, and the others agree upon some object in the room. The outsider has to discover that object by questions, which the insiders must answer only by "Yes" or "No." The task might seem hopeless, but a sharp child will unearth the secret in a few minutes. And once you allow yourself to be interviewed by a clever pressman your silence may be as expressive as words. A Harley Street friend of mine, who was attending Mr. Gladstone in his last illness, had an experience which exemplifies this. On leaving his patient's house one day a journalist accosted him, and walked a few hundred yards with him, plying him with questions about the illness which the nation was watching with anxiety. My friend never uttered a word except a "Yes" to one question; but the report of that "interview" filled twenty lines of the newspaper next day.

In a case of this kind there are only two ways of escape. One is to insult the journalist by treating him as we treat a professional beggar, and refusing to talk to him or even to listen to him. The other way is that which Mark Twain has patented. For the benefit of any who may not know that great humourist's story, I will give an illustrative case to explain his method. At a time when all England was interested in the matter, a well-known pressman, who represented an important News Agency, accosted me outside my office door with the question, "Are you sending an officer for Jabez Balfour?" Now, if we had decided not to send for the man, there could be no possible reason for refusing to say so. Therefore such a reply as "You mustn't ask me that question" would have been equivalent to saying "Yes." And yet secrecy was of special importance in the case. So I invited my questioner to come to my room, and I gave him an elaborate account of the action I meant to take, and of my reasons for taking it. But as he was leaving I followed him to the door, and as I shook hands with him I said that there was one thing more which I thought he ought to know, and that was that there was not a single word of truth in what I had told him! It was not my trick, but the expression of his face which made me explode with laughter as I re-entered my room and shut the door.

But what need was there to make any mystery in such a matter? At a friend's table I had met a gentleman from the Argentine, a near relative of a leading member of the Government, and from him I received many useful hints, indicating that secrecy was desirable. Though the Government in Buenos Ayres could not refuse the demand for the extradition of the accused, the man was a thousand miles away from the capital, and the Provincial authorities had no intention of letting him go. But the resourceful police officer to whom the case was entrusted outmanœuvred them in a clever plot to thwart both our Government and their own. Judgment had been obtained against Balfour on civil process for debt, and the game was to seize him under a commitment order of the Provincial Court as soon as he was handed over on the extradition charge. Accordingly the prisoner was not given up until the daily train for Buenos Ayres had started. But my Inspector, having made friends with the station-master, had arranged for a "special." And yet he escaped only by a few minutes; and before the train had covered more than three or four miles it was intercepted by the sheriff's officer, who rode out on the line, waving his writ, and signalling to them to stop. But the Inspector had taken the precaution of travelling on the engine, and he at once got between the driver and his levers, and the unfortunate sheriff was cut down by the train.

This, however, was only one chapter in the story. At a junction on the line, where a change of trains was necessary, the police had received orders by telegraph to arrest all concerned, on a charge of homicide. But as my officer was facing the driver when the accident occurred, he saw nothing of it; and while this difficulty was under discussion he quietly got his prisoner into the second "special" which was waiting for him, and started for the coast. I may add that the relatives of the unfortunate sheriff's officer received compensation for his death.

It will be seen, therefore, that it was not without reason that I sought to baffle my journalistic acquaintance when he tried to draw me in this case. And, by the way, I have a sequel to that story. One evening shortly afterwards I was dining with the Queen's Guard at St. James's Palace, when a report was brought to me that a dynamite explosion had taken place in a court off the Strand. I sent a note to the Chief Inspector of Explosives asking him to meet me there, and our inspection satisfied us that the event was a common gas explosion. As Sir Vivian Majendie and I passed out through the cordon of police that surrounded the place, my pressman friend came forward to ask if there was anything I could tell him about the case. I gave him the facts at once, and the result of our investigation of them. Finding presently that he was following us, I stopped again to see what he wanted. His meek appeal gave me another hearty laugh. "I beg your pardon, sir," said he, "but was it true what you told me just now?" I assured him that if he applied to me, as he had done then, to know whether I had anything to say about a case, I should alway deal frankly with him; but if he plied me with fishing questions I would fool him to the top of his bent. I played the same game with others, and with excellent results.

From an official point of view, of course, all this was grossly improper. I ought to have snubbed all pressmen and had them "chucked out," treating them in fact as the Cabinet Ministers have treated the suffragettes. And they would naturally have declared war upon me, to the detriment of my work, whereas I had not a single enemy among the journalists of London.

CHAPTER XIII

Some Scotland Yard stories—Lord Justice A. L. Smith and a girl's fictions—The escapades of a girl in boy's clothes—A chance incident gives a clue to a murder case—An Indian and his landlady's daughter—A trafficking case at Holloway Prison—The Colonial Office and a Boer informant—A strange divorce case—Finding a criminal wanted by the Paris police—Finding a fugitive husband—People who think they are watched by the police—People tortured by electric currents—Lunatics and Royalty—Mr. Gladstone's escape in 1893.

PEOPLE seem to appreciate "Scotland Yard Stories"; and as my avowed object in writing these pages is to interest and amuse, I give the following narratives which illustrate certain phases of Police work, and exemplify some strange types of human nature.

A street quarrel between two young men one night in February, 1896, attracted the attention of the police constable on the beat; and when they separated, one of them, whose action excited his suspicions, was brought to the station. There the delinquent was found to be a young woman in man's dress ; and when she appeared before a magistrate next morning, her story, which he heard in his private room, was so interesting and pathetic that, in discharging her, he directed that her case should be specially reported to me. It transpired, moreover, that she had received sympathy and pecuniary help from people in a very exalted position in London. Accordingly I sent for her. When she came to my office she was dressed neatly and with taste, in female garb, of course. She was attractive and ladylike, and rather pretty ; her voice was pleasing and her smile was charming. She sat facing me at the opposite side of my table for nearly an hour, talking over her wonderful life-story. By temperament and training I am a hopeless sceptic, but neither by word nor gesture did I betray my doubts about her narrative. Again and again I brought her round to various points in her story, and quietly cross-questioned her upon them. But her statements never varied; she never prevaricated, and a guileless child could not have answered me more promptly and simply.

The circumstances of her early life, she said, were long a mystery to her. Though the woman she supposed to be her mother was only a housekeeper, she was sent to a good school, and had occasional trips to the Continent. It was not till recent years that she discovered her real parentage. Her mother was a lady, and her father was the Lord Justice A. L. Smith. People of high degree who knew her story had been kind to her, and she had received valuable presents from them, notably some old furniture and a few valuable paintings. Among the people she named, who were personally known to me, she had much to say about Lord and Lady Rosebery; and she was very pathetic about the mingled kindness and neglect with which her father, the Lord Justice, had treated her.

The only item in her narrative which was capable of immediate verification I found to be true, namely, her possession of the old furniture and the paintings. But still I was sceptical. I knew that my friend, Mr. J. L. Wharton, then M.P. for Durham, was on terms of brotherly intimacy with "A.L." (as he always called him); so to him I applied. He scouted the story; and next day they called on me together. "I hear you have found a new daughter for me," was the Lord Justice's cheery greeting; "I hope she's pretty." I told him she was both pretty and charming. That, he declared, was clear evidence that she was his child; and yet there was not a word of truth in her statements.

I then pursued my inquiries, and I found that her story was fiction from first to last. Her father kept a bric-à-brac shop; and, as she lived near by, he used her lodgings as a temporary receptacle for some of his wares, including the "valuable pictures" of which she spoke. Her schooling was such as Mr. W. E. Forster's Education Act had provided, and her trips abroad were flights of fancy. Scores of times I have seen a truthful witness break down under the sort of cross-examination which this girl bore without wincing, and without making a single slip. I have had experience of similar cases, but this was incomparably the most interesting and extraordinary I have ever known.

Young women are the strangest of creatures, and their actual doings are sometimes more improbable than anything in the pages of fiction. It is not a capital felony for a woman to wear a man's clothes, but under the Metropolitan Police Acts disorderly proceedings of this kind are risky. And this made a certain Londoner very uneasy when his daughter took to this habit. So he came to see me privately, and put me in possession of the facts. It was then only an occasional freak with the girl, but presently it became habitual; and in changing her dress she also changed her name and became "William."

I omit some chapters of the story, for I will not risk disclosing the identity of the family concerned; but it ended in her going to America with another young woman—Matilda I will call her. I advised both families that if they wished their daughters to return to them they should avoid all agony-column appeals, and treat the matter in the most prosaic way. And the result justified my forecast. Two of Matilda's letters were shown to me. The first announced that Willie had proposed to her, and they were going to be married at once. The next, written a few weeks later, complained that Willie had treated her very badly. He had deserted her and gone away, and she begged for money to enable her to come home! And in due course a similar appeal came from Willie. These are plain facts: could any one venture to tell such a story in a sixpenny novel?

The day I was called to the Bar, one of the Masters of the High Court, the father of my friend from childhood—the late Lord Justice Fitzgibbon—gave me some kindly and useful counsel. One piece of advice I never forgot; it was to keep my eyes and ears open, and I should often find that the chance incidents and information of daily life would prove useful in practice at the Bar. The importance of this in Police work could scarcely be exaggerated. I will illustrate what I mean.

After a hurried dinner one evening, I went off to address a meeting of the Y.M.C.A. During the singing of a hymn, the chairman intimated to me that the next item on the programme was my address. But at that moment one of my Inspectors entered the hall, and I saw at a glance that it was not for ghostly counsel he had come. I told the chairman that I must go out for a few minutes; and, followed by my Inspector, I left the hall. He had omitted to submit a report in a criminal case that morning, and his object in coming to me was to escape being brought before me next morning as a defaulter. The matter itself was insignificant—it was only a petty case of fraud. A schoolboy had called on a clergyman living near London, and had obtained a sovereign from him on the pretence that he had lost his purse, and wanted money to enable him to reach the house of a relative in Hampshire. But the clergyman ascertained that the lad, instead of going south, had booked north by the L. & N.W. Railway.

I granted the officer the relief he sought, and returned to the hall to give my lecture. But this report gave me the first clue I had obtained to the solution of a London murder case. The fraud was committed the morning after the murder; and I had received a letter from a girl friend in the town to which the lad had booked, in which she mentioned incidentally that he had been to see them, and that he seemed to have "gone dotty," as his head was full of some murder he had committed in London. After my lecture I gave the order for his arrest; and the case happily ended in an acquittal on the ground of insanity.

There was no amusement to be got out of that case. It was sad and tragic. But Scotland Yard is looked upon as a sort of universal inquiry office, and the strangest appeals are made to the Police. About the time of the murder last mentioned, I had a visit from a woman who wanted me to prevent her daughter from marrying an Indian law student who had been living in her house as a lodger. My attendant brought me word that she would see no one but the chief; and she seemed so very respectable, and so mysterious withal, that he thought her business must be important. When I let her in, and heard her story, the very impudence of her coming to me took my fancy. She told me that everything she said to her daughter only made the girl more determined to marry the lodger; but she felt sure I could prevent it. "Who is he?" I asked; and I found that he was a man whom I knew personally. I told her to bring her daughter to see me, stipulating that I must see the girl alone.

They came next day, and I sent the mother into my ante-room. The girl was a perky chit, and she showed at once that she had made up her mind not to be influenced by anything I said. So, after a few questions, to which she snapped back pert answers, I told her that I did not at all agree with her mother about her *fiancé*. He had been introduced to me by my friend Lord Blank, and I thought him a very nice fellow indeed. As I went on to say all the kind things I could of him, her hard face changed, and her eyes beamed. But as she was leaving the room I stopped her, and added in a casual way that there was one thing more I ought to say to her: of course she would not object to her husband taking a second wife when he returned home to India. She flared up at once, and talked about killing herself. But, I urged, his father was a man of wealth and high position, and he would certainly be annoyed at his son's bringing home an English Christian wife; and he would never rest till he got him to marry some native woman of his own rank. The end of it all was that when the girl rejoined her mother she announced her intention to break off the engagement that very day.

This was merely a chance incident, and a study in human nature. But shortly afterwards I had a somewhat similar case, which illustrates the dovetailing of private with official matters in Police work. This time my visitor was my old friend Lady Blank, who came to tell me that her favourite niece had become engaged to a scamp, and she wanted my counsel and help. The scamp was a man of good family, who had held a commission in a crack regiment; but he had been convicted of a fraud, and was then serving a sentence in Holloway Prison. And the niece was a charming girl, and such an accomplished musician that she was independent of her father. And the appeals of her people only led to her leaving home, and setting up in lodgings by herself. I promised my friend to take action if I could trust her not to let her niece know of her visit to me.

That morning I had received a private note from Sir Evelyn Ruggles-Brise about a case of trafficking at Holloway. They suspected some "gentleman prisoner," but the case had completely baffled them. Could I help them? I sent for one of the shrewdest of my Inspectors, and showing him Sir Evelyn's note, I gave him the girl's name and address, with directions to call upon her and tell her I was going to arrest her for the offence. "If," said I, "you find I am on a wrong tack, back out at once; but if the shot tells, frighten her out of her life, and advise her to come to me immediately and to throw herself on my mercy."

Within a couple of hours she was seated in my room. She pleaded that she had befriended the prisoner because he had been hardly treated, and everybody was against him. Of course I was not supposed to know of her engagement, so I gave her credit for the best of motives; but, I added, a pretty girl was not the right sort of person to befriend a man of his character—I knew a good deal about him—and the question before me was whether I could condone an offence for which she was liable to six months' hard labour; would she promise me to hold no further communication of any kind with the prisoner? This led her tearfully to tell me of her engagement to him. I was duly shocked, and I put it to herself to decide whether, in view of this, I could possibly trust her not to repeat the offence. But I went on to say, six months' hard labour was a trifle in comparison with her fate as the wife of such a man; and I gave her two facts about his antecedents, of which I had definite knowledge.

To make a long story short, she ended by promising to break with him, and to tell him her decision as soon as he came out of prison. No, no, she must break with him at once, and by letter. But, she pleaded, she must see him, for he had left his watch and trinkets and purse with her. This I would not hear of. I told her to think over the matter ; and, if she decided to act on my advice, to bring me the man's property and the letter I wished her to write. Twenty-four hours afterwards the property was at Scotland Yard and the letter was at the prison.

The girl's next visit, several months afterwards, was to thank me cordially for having saved her. And in the following year she again became engaged, with the full approval of her parents, and she married well and happily. Not till then did I let her know that her aunt was an old pal of mine, and that my officer's visit was "a put-up job." And if the Chairman of the Prison Department should chance to read these pages, he will learn for the first time how it was that I put an end to that Holloway Prison trafficking case.

This was by no means the only instance in

which a private friend gave me help that was useful to me officially. A case of the kind, which occurred during the Boer War, is worth telling. A friend brought me one day a document which he believed to be a copy of an important report prepared for the Boer Government by one of their agents. A "lady typist" whom he had formerly employed had, by his assistance, been set up in the business, and he had further befriended her by giving her work, and recommending her office. A mysterious stranger had called upon her with a document which he wanted typed immediately; and as it was very confidential he asked to be allowed to remain in her office while it was being done. Her womanly curiosity being thus aroused, she surreptitiously took a duplicate copy; and this she brought to my friend, who, after glancing through it, drove to Scotland Yard and handed it to me. He asked me to keep it in my hands, and not to use the information it contained in any manner that would disclose the source from which it came to me.

I saw at once that the information was of value. So I embodied it in a private letter to Lord Selborne, who was then Under-Secretary at the Colonial Office. Lord Selborne was keenly appreciative, assuring me that I had given them particulars which they had been anxious to obtain. And next day he told me that information entirely confirming what I had given him had reached the Colonial Office from another quarter. I guessed in a moment that the "other quarter" was the original report on a copy of which my letter was based; but, of course, I was bound to keep faith with my friend, and not to betray the typist. It became embarrassing, however, when Lord Selborne went on to say that they wished to recompense my informant. I promised to consider the matter, and to see him again. But when I conferred with my friend, he told me that he had already rewarded his *protégée* and he did not wish anything further to be said about it. Here was a double mystery: that I could obtain such reliable and useful news about the Boers, and this from some one who refused a reward!

Fiction palls upon any one who has a behind-the-scenes acquaintance with the facts of real life. At a luncheon-table one day the late Mr. Justice Butt began to banter me about my official work; and I turned the tables on him by disclosing the facts of a recent divorce case, for the judge was attached to that branch of the High Court. When Douglas Jerrold's wife reminded him of her birthday, and that she was then forty, he suggested that he ought to be allowed to treat her as a banknote, and change her for two twenties. The "villain" of my story —Jones by name—was not quite so Oriental; but having become engaged to a rich widow, he naturally wished to get rid of his wife; and being a man of ingenuity and resource, he made use of the Divorce Court to that end. When I told my story, the Judge cynically remarked that though he had a high opinion of my literary powers, he had no idea that I was such a master of fiction; and he suggested that if I published my story in a shilling shocker I should make my reputation in that line. Next day, however, he discovered that the case to which I had referred had been tried by the President of the Court; and he wrote to me to urge that I ought not to disclose the facts. But only good can come of telling the story now.

Jones's application for divorce was based on a written confession by his wife that she had been unfaithful to him, her paramour being his own brother George. The brother George was not altogether a myth, for Jones had had such a brother, but he had died in childhood. The wife had received a petty legacy, and she signed her "confession" unread, believing it to be an application to the Probate Court to enable her to get the money. The "decree nisi" was a matter of course, and six months afterwards it was made absolute, Jones having intercepted process upon his wife by the same artifice as before. For he had been living peacefully with her all this time; and when he now left her in order to marry the widow, she duly saw him off at the railway terminus from which he started, and parted from him with a fond kiss. Not even in such a detail as this am I romancing; it was a part of her statement to a Scotland Yard officer from whom she received the first intimation that she was a divorced woman. And then it was that the Police obtained knowledge of his crime. For the object of the officer's visit to her was merely to discover what had become of the man.

He had been at one time employed on some private Secret Service work, though neither the Police nor I had any knowledge of him. His method seems to have been to employ a number of satellites, setting each of them to watch the others as dangerous conspirators. Now even a trained expert finds it difficult to do watching duty without attracting notice and exciting suspicion about his own movements. And with amateurs it is impossible. Therefore the more carefully these fellows did the work assigned to them, the more sensational were their reports. And the fraud was not discovered till their paymaster disappeared, and one and another of them came to Scotland Yard to ask about him, and to seek further employment in the same line.

Jones was a proficient French scholar, and with his new wife's money he took a good house in Paris, and advertised that he would receive a few sons of gentlemen, to whom he promised a good education, "with high moral training." So particular was he about his pupils being real gentlemen, that he refused an application from the head of one of our great Oxford Street shops. His taking up this line gave me my chance, for I was determined to bring him to book. His offence was not extraditable, and as long as he remained on the other side of the Channel he was safe. But though I angled for him for some time in vain, I caught him at last, and he was convicted and sentenced.

A successful coup in Police work is sometimes only a fluke. By a mere chance I gained the firm friendship of M. Goron, who, when I first went to Scotland Yard, was head of the *Sureté*, or Detective Police of Paris—a friendship that was of great value to me in my official work. An important criminal had eluded him and escaped to London. The case was one of such gravity that M. Goron came over in person to enlist all the help I could afford in capturing the fugitive. He called upon me to give me the particulars, but the only particulars available afforded no clue whatever to the man's associates or movements in London. He could not tell me even by what route he had travelled from Paris. In a word, he left me absolutely nothing to work upon except a photograph of the delinquent. "You want me then to find this man among the 7,000,000 of people in London," said I with a laugh, "nothing could be easier, I'll get him for you!"

It seemed an utterly hopeless quest; but I gave directions that all the officers should study the photograph on the chance of their coming upon the man in the course of their ordinary duties. A couple of hours later I despatched a note to M. Goron to tell him that his man was in custody at Scotland Yard. His gratification was lost in his amazement at such a result. "But how do you do it?" he exclaimed, "we can't do that sort of thing in Paris." I confess that I was guilty of the duplicity of concealing the fact that it was a sheer fluke. Two of the C.I.D. Inspectors met the man on the Strand and recognised him as the original of the photograph.

When M. Goron next visited London he enlisted

my help in a case that was quite outside the sphere of Police work. A pretty little Portuguese lady, whose husband had gone off with another woman, followed the couple to Paris, and M. Goron had interested himself on her behalf, and ascertained that they were in London. As he was coming here on official business, he brought the lady to my office, and appealed to me to find the husband. I gave him the same answer as on the previous occasion ; but in a few hours we located the fugitives in a lodging-house in Bayswater.

In this case, however, success was due to legitimate Police inquiries. On their arrival in London one piece of their luggage was missing, and the fuss they naturally made about it attracted notice to them. M. Goron's admiration of our skill was as generous and unreserved as on the previous occasion. And if I did not tell him how the man was found, my reticence was due to reluctance to hurt his feelings. Our Police are the friends of the people, and therefore the people are always ready to help us. But it is not so in Paris. Indeed I am not sure that it can be said of any other country in the world ; and the way this operates in a case like that above mentioned, is that everybody, whether railway porter, cabman, or man in the street, is generally willing to assist the Police.

People who Think they are Watched

If it be often difficult to find people who are wanted by the Police, it is sometimes more difficult to get rid of people who think they are wanted. Such is the pressure of life nowadays, that people are apt to "go dotty" in various ways; and the disease often shows itself by a delusion that the victim of it is being watched by the Police. The vigilance of an all-seeing Providence is not more inexorable than that of Scotland Yard in the estimation of such a man! He cannot look out of his window without seeing a Police agent lurking somewhere near his house. He cannot go out, day or night, but that his steps are dogged. If he takes a railway journey, a detective gets into the next compartment just as the train is starting; and when he alights at his destination another detective is waiting for him on the station platform.

For some years after I left office, I received letters from dupes of this delusion, appealing to me to use my influence with my successor on their behalf. And my assurance that it was all a delusion sometimes brought me a sheaf of closely written pages of diary, detailing the victim's movements day after day, and the proofs of his being thus persecuted. One man stares at him, and, as he passes, another man "shuffles with his feet"—a not uncommon element in the craze. I can recall only one instance in which an official reply proved of any use. It was the case of a personal friend of mine. I told his brother to write to me about it, and in reply I expressed regret at the annoyance caused him and added that I had given the necessary orders to put an end to it, as he had been mistaken for some one else.

Judging by official correspondence, this delusion is a speciality with *men*. A not uncommon phase of the disease with women is the belief that they are being constantly subjected to a powerful electric current, worked by some one in a neighbouring house. If a real infliction of this kind were possible, the victims would not suffer more than do the dupes of this delusion. I never hesitate to ridicule the fears of men who thus suppose they are shadowed by the Police, but these poor creatures excite only pity. And while it is useless to reason with them, to help them is impossible.

If folk of this sort are only to be pitied, lunatics whose delusions have reference to Royalty are a danger. And it is remarkable how often mental aberration assumes this phase. This was a frequent cause of anxiety to the authorities, and of danger to the Sovereign, during all Queen Victoria's reign. When I first came to London a lunatic of this description gave the Police no little trouble. One morning when he had announced his intention of going to Windsor, where the Queen was in residence, three officers were set to watch him. He got up steam by a couple of rounds of Hyde Park at five miles an hour, and then headed for Windsor. One of the officers broke down before they had gone many miles; another was done before they were half way; and the third, who stuck to his man, was invalided for a week afterwards. But by the time the lunatic reached the Castle, the exercise had so soothed him that he quietly took train back to town. This sort of thing it was that precluded charging him before a magistrate, for in this free country it is not illegal to take a twenty-mile walk at five miles an hour.

Shortly afterwards Superintendent Williamson[1] called on him to see what he could make of him. He found the man in a state of great excitement, with a huge pulpit Bible open before him. He had just made the momentous discovery that he was the Messiah! Williamson urged on him that it was extremely wrong to keep the discovery to himself: he ought to make it known. But how? "Come to Bow Street, and tell it to the Chief

[1] See p. 125, *ante*.

Magistrate in open Court, and it will be published in every newspaper in London." The man responded eagerly, and was ready in a moment. "But," said Williamson, "you mustn't go without that Bible." A few minutes brought them to Bow Street in a hansom, and the poor fellow's dramatic announcement was followed, of course, by his committal to an asylum.

The public never realised what a marvellous escape Mr. Gladstone had in April, 1893, when the lunatic Townsend, with a loaded revolver in his pocket, lay in wait for him in Downing Street. A lunatic is often diverted from his purpose as easily as a child; and the man's own explanation of his failing to fire was that the Premier smiled at him when passing into No. 10—a providential circumstance that, for Mr. Gladstone was not addicted to smiling. That case cost me much distress of mind. "Never keep a document," should be the first rule with a criminal. "Never destroy a document," should be an inexorable rule in Police work. But in this case I had destroyed a letter that would have proved an important piece of evidence. I always ignored threatening letters myself, and I have had my share of them; and when one of my principal subordinates brought me a letter threatening his life, I felt so indignant and irritated at the importance he attached to it, and the fuss he made over it, that I threw it into the fire. That letter was from Townsend, and though no harm came of my act, I could not forgive myself for it.

CHAPTER XIV

C.I.D. officers at Channel Ports—The theft of the Gainsborough picture—The Channel gang of thieves, and their fate—Home Office schemes on behalf of such criminals, thwarted by the "humanitarians"—Criminals and how to protect ourselves against them—A Ross-shire story—Various hints—The dropped trinket fraud—The painted bird fraud—Photograph enlargements—Cheap jewellery—A Father Healy story—The "O.U. Duck" brooch.

When I say that the head of the Criminal Investigation Department is never off duty, I do not mean, of course, that he is tied to his office-room. A "nervous breakdown," involving complete cessation from work, would not be as common as it is if people were more discreet and intelligent about themselves. As already hinted, I was in danger of such a collapse when I went to Scotland Yard, and for some years I had to be careful. "I sleeps well and I eats well," said the tramp, "but when anybody torks about work I gets all of a tremble. And yet work will not really hurt any one who can eat and sleep. But a bout of insomnia, even for a single night, was always a danger-signal with me, and I eased off next day. In such circumstances, if I could arrange to leave town for a day, a trip across the Channel proved an unfailing remedy. I thus secured some hours of uninterrupted work in the train journeys, and some hours of play between times, and on the following day I was fit for double duty.

My Channel trips, moreover, had a business side to them. During the dynamite campaign Scotland Yard officers were stationed at various home and foreign ports ; and at certain places, as, for instance, at Dover and Calais, and Folkestone and Boulogne, their presence had proved of such value to the public that it was decided to continue their services. A criminal named Powell (he was Raymond's accomplice in the theft of Mr. Agnew's Gainsborough picture) was one of a gang that for years had lived in luxury on the contents of purses and pocket-books stolen on the Channel boats. It needs no great powers of imagination to realise what it means for a paterfamilias to land in France with his party minus their railway tickets and the money for their sojourn in Switzerland or on the Riviera. And M. Favre, who, while Stationmaster at Calais, was the friend of every British traveller, told me that sometimes there were half a dozen cases of this kind in a single day, whereas after the C.I.D. officer was stationed at the port there were not half a dozen cases in the year. This was an inestimable boon to the public, and yet it was only by constant watchfulness and some diplomacy that I was able to ensure the continuance of the arrangement; for any lapse on the part of the officers, or the least friction with the local police, would have made it impossible. Hence the importance of paying surprise visits to the ports.

I have mentioned Powell, the professional thief, and the sequel of his story is worth telling. The raids of his gang upon the purses and pocket-books on the Channel boats were worth hundreds of pounds a year to them. But they had another "lay" that brought them in thousands at times. Valuable securities of a bulky nature, passing from London to Paris, are entrusted to the railway companies; and the boats have a treasure-chest in which such parcels are deposited when crossing the Channel. So perfect is the organisation of professional thieving, that these men were able to obtain particulars of consignments of this kind, and to procure keys for the treasure-chests. They were able thus to substitute dummy parcels for the originals, and to get away with their booty before their crime was discovered. I got word one day that the gang meant to get hold of a parcel of bonds which a well-known Insurance Company was sending to Paris on a certain night. By inquiry in the City I ascertained that the Company named was in fact sending the securities, as reported to me. Accordingly I despatched officers to Dover and Calais to deal with the case; and the men were seized on landing at Calais. But the bonds were still safe in the treasure-chest.

The French Police were amazed to find three well-dressed "gentlemen," with gold watches and alberts, brought in as if they were pickpockets. And they were horrified when my officers seized one of the "gentlemen" by the throat and forced open his jaws, to secure a bit of paper they had seen him putting into his mouth. It was a railway cloak-room ticket for a portmanteau, which was found to contain some £2,000 worth of coupons stolen by the gang on a former occasion. There was also found upon him a key of the treasure-chest of the boat which ought to have crossed that night, and a wax impression of the corresponding key for the boat which actually made the trip. Captain Morgan,

R.N., who was then Marine Superintendent at Dover, had a theory that the older boats were the best for bad weather; and thus it came about that on the night in question the regular boat had not made the crossing; and so the thieves were thwarted, as was also Scotland Yard.

Here was an object-lesson in the crime problem. These men, as I have said, held £2,000 worth of the securities stolen in their last haul, and we found as much more in their lodgings. To men of their class such a heap of money was wealth. They could have lived upon it in luxury for many a year. If, therefore, they crossed the Channel on a stormy night, to raid the treasure-chest of the steamer, it was not because of the pressure of want, but because they were professional thieves and outlaws. Did we not believe in a future life, we should urge that such men should be shot at sight, like wild beasts, or strung up to the nearest lamp-posts. And yet it was in the interests of criminals of this type that those troublesome cranks, the humanitarians, wrecked Mr. Herbert Gladstone's Prevention of Crimes Bill, under which they might have been kept in custody until they could give proof of real repentance and reform.

The three men were committed to prison in Boulogne. Yet we had not the needed evidence to sustain a demand for their extradition, and the French Police could make no charge against them. By utilising the influence of the railway companies, however, and appealing to headquarters in Paris, we succeeded in having them kept under lock and key for several months. The result was that divine justice prevailed where the human had failed. In Boulogne jail they were completely buried, and their friends here gave them up. Powell had left a blank cheque with his "wife," to be used in case a mishap befell him; and the woman cleared out his bank balance and went off with another man. Soon afterwards he died of want in the streets of Southampton. Another of the gang—"Shrimps" was his *nom de guerre*—was betrayed in the same way by his "wife"; and I heard that, his pockets weighted with stones, he had taken a last sea-trip, and had thrown himself overboard in mid-channel. What became of "Red Bob," the other member of the gang, I do not know. But unless he too has gone the way of all flesh, we may be sure that he is still "following his profession." For these professional criminals never change. During their spells of liberty they live in comfort, under the protection of the laws they systematically violate; and if and when they are convicted of crime, they receive a sentence of a few years' duration, and are then let loose again upon society. How long will the public tolerate this scandalous and stupid system?

If these men are the victims of neglect or harsh treatment in childhood—and this may possibly be true of some of them—it is no reason why they should be allowed to prey upon the community, to corrupt others by their evil example, and to breed children after their kind. It is all the more reason why they should be saved from themselves by being relegated to a "preventive detention," in which they might be taught to live a useful life, with hope not only of happiness in the next world, but also of restoration to liberty in this world, if and when they give proof of genuine repentance and reform.

Under such a system "Shrimps" and poor old Powell, who was not a bad fellow in his way, might to-day be living not unhappy lives in an asylum-prison, and there learning to hope for heaven hereafter. And this was the aim and purpose of the Prevention of Crimes Bill of 1908, which the pestilent influence of the humanitarians changed into a measure to make the way of transgressors easier than ever. Upon their heads be it if criminals of the Powell type remain a curse to society, and pass to their eternal doom without the opportunity for repentance, which an intelligent philanthropy would have secured to them.

I have no intention of discussing the graver side of the crime problem in these pages; but there are certain aspects of it which are of great practical interest to the general public. Why do we need to live behind bolts and bars, as if we were in an enemy's country? First, there is the element of professional crime, to which I have already referred, and of which I have written much elsewhere. We have in our midst a number—and a very limited number—of men who, as Sir Alfred Wills has aptly said, "follow crime as the business of their lives." We also have to deal with a much larger class of offenders, who vary the monotony of an ostensibly honest life by deliberately giving rein to their criminal propensities whenever a fitting opportunity offers. Then again, the vast and steadily increasing army of needy people includes a minority who are ready to replenish their purses or their larders by dishonest means. And lastly, we must take account of the chance crimes of people of weak moral fibre, who are carried away by sudden temptation. It concerns us all therefore to consider how we can protect ourselves against the dangers to which the presence of these actual or possible law-breakers exposes us.

I must begin by propounding the seemingly heartless thesis that people who suffer from crimes against property are very generally the victims of their own folly or greed. Of course there are exceptions. The statement does not usually apply to the work of men who are in the front rank as criminals; but fortunately front-rank men are as rare in this as in other professions. My friend, the late Major Arthur Griffiths, used to tell how, when he was in charge of one of our convict-prisons, he mislaid the key of the office safe one day, when the visiting director was hourly expected; so he told the Chief Warder to get one of the convicts to open it. But in that great prison only one man could be found who was competent to undertake the job, and he had been trained in the factory of one of our well-known manufacturers of safes. Of course a couple of navvies with pickaxes could break up any safe that ever was made; but if criminals went to work in that way they would arouse the whole neighbourhood. A good safe provides full security against ordinary thieves. If, therefore, a lady keeps £1,000 worth of jewels in a trinket box on the dressing-table, or in her wardrobe, is it cynical to say that she has herself to blame if she loses them? To spend £10 on a safe is not a very heavy insurance to pay in such a case.

But the best safe ever made will not give security if common care be lacking. I could tell of a certain lady who profited by a police warning, and used to boast of her Chubb. But one evening she left her keys lying on the table, and when she returned her safe was empty! Is there ever a jewel larceny perpetrated during a railway journey that is not due to carelessness of this kind? And women seem to be sillier even than men. Certain it is that they delight in flaunting their silliness.

A cynic whom I could name raises the question whether the sort of women who wear French heels have immortal souls. And he explains the hideous monstrosities of the illustrated advertisements of milliners and corset-makers by the theory that the trade is run by Jews, whose law forbids their making the likeness of anything in heaven above or on the earth beneath! But if men be less silly, they have less excuse for their silliness. For example, a man who passes through a crowd with a gold watch-chain exposed has himself to blame if he loses both chain and watch. I have seen more pick-pockets than most people; but I state a plain fact when I say that I never saw one except in custody. Yes, once I did. On the night of Queen Victoria's Jubilee I paraded the streets wearing a gorgeous chain that I had bought for sixpence in Fleet Street—there was a door-key at the pocket end of it—and twice that night a thief had a try for it.

A cynical classification of the population of the country as knaves or fools, sharps or flats, might seem smart and clever, but it would be quite unintelligent and false. For the Britisher is a peace-loving biped, and honest withal; and if we eliminate the element of the alien leaven in our midst, the volume of crime is marvellously small. Indeed, the twin curses of drink and gambling account for the great majority of the offences recorded in the criminal statistics.

During one of my first visits to a friend's summer residence in Ross-shire, I was startled one day at the luncheon-table by the exclamation, "Oh, there's the thief!" and I saw a fellow who might aptly be described as a human "lurcher," shuffling along the avenue which ran between the house and the sea-shore. My curiosity was excited by hearing a thief thus designated by the definite article, and my inquiries elicited that he was the only dishonest person in the district, and that, but for him, locks and bolts might be ignored. In the course of a country walk the next day I was asked to speak to *the* policeman, whose office, I was told, would be a sinecure but for the presence of the thief.

Here is one phase of the crime problem in miniature. I have already spoken of the expert professional criminals whose exploits tax the resources of a highly trained Police. They are few in number and well known to the Police. Indeed, there would be no difficulty in including their names in the Trades Section of the "Post Office London Directory"; and if common sense and genuine philanthropy were allowed a hearing, a few years would suffice to suppress the whole fraternity.

Happily, however, humble folk like myself and the great majority of my readers have but little to fear from these high-class professionals. They go for higher game; they play for higher stakes. But we have in our midst a number of people of criminal propensities and weak moral fibre, who will prey upon us if we give them a chance. Not a few of them are objects of pity, but our punishment-of-crime system is blindly pitiless. To revert to my Ross-shire story, one might suppose that a sane community would pension the policeman and relegate the thief to a detention in which he might lead a useful life. But, to quote an aphorism that now ranks as classical, the law is an ass and an idiot. Here is a case in the morning paper which lies before me as I write, of a criminal aged eighty-one who has spent more than half his life in jail, and who is once again sentenced at the Sessions. And his cheery words on leaving the dock make it plain that notwithstanding his fourscore years he contemplates returning again to his normal course of life. The man has the credit of being a good workman when he does work; and if as soon as he gave proof that he either could not, or would not, keep his hands from picking and stealing, he had been deprived of the liberty he always abuses, he might have lived a useful and not unhappy life in a humanely administered asylum prison. Such a discipline, moreover, might in time have so reformed the criminal as to make his discharge a benefit instead of being a curse to the community.

My purpose here, however, is not to expose and denounce the mingled stupidity and barbarity of our methods of dealing with law-breakers, but to indicate how we can best protect ourselves against their depredations. And here, I repeat, we usually need but common care. A sensible man will button up his coat in a crowd as automatically as he will open his umbrella in a shower.

And a lady who can't "button up" will avoid a crowd if she is wearing trinkets that can be "sneaked." And if people must needs carry money, a very simple precaution will afford immunity. Cut bank-notes in two, and carry the several halves in separate receptacles, and the sneak thief will be thwarted. And then as regards our houses. A high-class burglar can crack any crib in spite of locks and bolts; but high-class burglars are few, and ordinary precautions will give security against ordinary operators. But it is useless to lock the front door if the back door be left on the latch, or to bar all the windows except one.

It may seem intolerable that in a civilised country we should need to live thus in a state of siege. But pending the introduction of more sensible and humane methods of dealing with criminals, we must reconcile ourselves to it. For while the common tramp thief is a poor creature whom careful and shrewd people may ignore, we must reckon with a small army of clever folk whose perverted mental activity is exercised at the expense of their neighbours.

And, as I have said, it is not folly only that gives them their opportunities: greed has often still more to do with it. Among the petty frauds to which this remark applies, the "dropped trinket" is a case in point. This used to be very popular. You see it lying on the pavement, but, before you can reach it, an out-at-elbows fellow picks it up and pockets it. Then he timidly pulls it out again and offers to sell it for a few shillings, for he is in dire need and wants to get food for his starving family. The thing needs to be done furtively, for "larceny by finding" is an offence known to the criminal law. But "greed of gain" prevails, and the dupe pays five shillings for a ring or bauble which the thief bought for sixpence.

The painted bird fraud, again, owes its success to the same baneful influence; and here the same mean element comes in, for the dupe thinks he is over-reaching the poor fellow who does not know the value of a songbird. The following story was told both of Sir Henry Hawkins and of Sir James Mathew, but I cannot say whether it was true of either of them. It is worth telling all the same. Appealed to by the rascal to tell him what kind of a bird it was he had caught, the Judge replied, after taking a good look at his questioner, "Well, having regard to the old proverb about 'birds of a feather,' I should say it was a jail bird!"

There are some photographers so full of benevolence that, without fee or reward, they will make a beautiful enlargement of any photograph entrusted to them. But the picture is such a work of art that it would savour of profanity to risk its being injured by failing to provide a good frame for it, and this will be supplied at cost price. A rascal carried on this fraud in Paris during my reign at Scotland Yard, and for aught I know he may be at it still. He was cunning enough to send the promised enlargement to a few well-known people unconditionally; and these became decoys for others who, if they refused to forward the price demanded for the frame, failed even to secure the return of their own photograph, or to get an answer to their letters of remonstrance or appeal.

Then again we have in our midst philanthropists who are so devoured by love to their neighbours, that they will send you a beautiful watch, a perfect timekeeper, of course, as a free gift; and the only acknowledgment they look for is that you will buy a suitable chain from them at cost price. You send the cash, and the articles you receive in exchange are such as you might buy for less money in any shop that sells flash trinkets. The watch is full of wheels, of course, and they go round with more or less regularity; or if they stop you have the satisfaction of knowing that the hands mark the time with absolute accuracy once in every twelve hours!

A good story is told of two great Irishmen, both of whom are now gone from us, the late Archbishop Plunket and Father Healy, the well-known parish priest of Bray. Making their way together to Bray railway station one morning, the priest urged that they should hurry, but the prelate's appeal to his watch convinced him that they had ample time. They arrived to see the train for Dublin disappearing. The Archbishop's apologies were lavish. He pleaded that he had always had unbounded faith in his watch. "My dear Lord Plunket," was Father Healy's rejoinder, "faith won't do without the good works." Will people who answer these fraudulent advertisements please note.

My reference to the "dropped trinket" fraud reminds me of a personal incident that gave me much amusement at the time. One morning on my way to Scotland Yard, I picked up a brooch in Kensington Gardens. It was a prominent object as it sparkled in the sunshine in the middle of the path, and I took for granted it had been dropped by either of the two nursemaids who were walking ahead of me. They were the only human beings in sight; for it is extraordinary how few people use these beautiful parks on a winter morning. The trinket was what is called an "O.U. duck" brooch, the vowels being intertwined in a cipher, with a little gilt duck underneath—an ornament that was at one time very popular with girls of a certain class. When I overtook the first of these nursemaids, she told me at once that she did not wear a brooch. When I came up to the other girl and asked her whether she had dropped a brooch, she answered as promptly, "I think so, sir, what kind is it?" If I had produced the brooch that girl would certainly have said it was hers. But with a stolid face, and in a leaden tone of voice I replied, "O.U. duck." "O, you go along," she exclaimed with a toss of her head, as she jerked herself away. On arrival at my office I gave the brooch and the story to my Superintendent; and within twenty minutes the trinket was in the Lost Property branch, and the story was in every branch of the Commissioner's office.

CHAPTER XV

A £20,000 fraud—Count Schouvaloff's sham informant—A bogus plot to destroy warships—The "confidence trick"—The "Spanish prisoner" fraud—The American "gold brick" swindle—Gambling clubs in London—Raid upon a club in St. James's—Improper literature: action of the Post Office and the Home Office.

THE offences I have been describing are of a very petty kind, and my readers may wish to hear about frauds perpetrated by criminals of a higher class. I am perhaps the only living person unconnected with the great City house to which the following story relates, who has knowledge of what I am about to narrate. It is a house whose name is in high repute in all the capitals of Europe. A genius claimed to have discovered the secret of making gold, and he offered to sell it to the firm in question. By means of a process which he had discovered, the bulk of any quantity of gold could be increased by one-half, at trifling expense. His dupes accepted his terms, subject to his giving proof of the value of his discovery; and to test it they proposed to supply him with a hundred sovereigns and the needed plant. He "thought scorn" of working on such a petty sum as that; it would be waste of time, for the process was a tedious one. Finally it was arranged that he should have £20,000 in sovereigns; and a house was taken in Leman Street, Whitechapel, and there a laboratory was fitted up for his use. The gold was placed in tanks provided for the purpose; the needed chemicals were supplied; and the experiment proceeded, with elaborate precautions against larceny or fraud. The man was emphatic in insisting on two points: no one but himself was to enter the laboratory; and he was to be rigorously searched every time he passed out.

After many weeks, during which his visits were frequent, he disappeared; and when eventually the door was forced, the tanks which had contained the gold were empty, and the bottles which contained the chemicals were full. What had become of the £20,000? No one but an expert has any conception of the bulk and weight of such a sum of money. And the fullest inquiry only served to elicit proof that thė man had been searched with exemplary care at every visit. The mystery might have remained for ever unsolved if the criminal had not himself supplied the solution of it. In sheer bravado and pride in his achievement, he wrote to the firm he had swindled, telling them of his appreciation of the money, and of his confidence that they would rather lose it than incur ridicule on every Exchange in Europe by a prosecution which would disclose their folly. And then he revealed his method. Every time he left the laboratory that gold-headed cane he carried was packed with sovereigns!

"International criminals" of this type are men of extraordinary cleverness and dash. Before coming to England as Ambassador, Count Schouvaloff was head of the Political Police at St. Petersburg—the "Third Section," I believe they call it. There was no man in Europe who was less likely to be victimised by a swindler, and yet he was duped by one of these rascals. When returning from the Continent one day he got into conversation with a fellow-passenger on the Channel boat—a man of good address, well-spoken, well-groomed, and of charming manners. He told the Ambassador that he had just been to Spain on a Secret

Service mission of much difficulty and delicacy, and he was in high spirits at his success. And he mentioned in an off-hand way that he had got on the track of the forgers who were then flooding Russia with counterfeit rouble-notes. Forgeries of this kind have been a constant cause of grave trouble and loss to the Russian Government, and the Count took the bait, and asked the fellow to call upon him.

When he called at the Embassy he freely gave particulars about the gang, adding incidentally, and in his grandest manner, that one of the men had dropped a hint that he was ready to betray his companions, but he would need a very big bribe. To any one versed in Secret Service work there was nothing to excite suspicion in his refusal to be put in touch with one of the Ambassador's agents. It was only a pleasure, however, to give his Excellency every help possible. The Count asked whether he would undertake the mission himself. This he was very reluctant to do. The men would probably be found where he left them the week before; but, on the other hand, he might have to follow them half across Europe, and possibly to Russia, involving such a long absence from London as would seriously prejudice his regular work. But at last he yielded, and he left the Embassy with a cheque for £1,000 in his pocket.

Having regard to the magnitude of the losses incurred by the Russian Government by rouble-note forgeries, the expenditure of £1,000 in such a business was a mere trifle. But after the man left the Embassy the Ambassador's suspicions began to awaken; and half an hour after his signing the cheque, the Bank had orders to stop payment of it. It was too late. The swindler had already drawn the money; and neither the Russian Embassy nor Scotland Yard ever got on his track.

Now a fellow who could successfully play a game of this kind with such a man as Count Schouvaloff must possess a combination of qualities that would insure success in almost any position in life. Some years ago a genius of this type levied heavy toll upon half the Chancelleries of Europe, by warning them of plots to destroy warships by means of bombs disguised as lumps of coal. I was known and trusted by the staff of several of the Foreign Embassies, and in this way I heard privately of the man's doings in other European capitals before he turned up in London. The first day he called upon me there was no suggestion on his part of demanding, or even of needing, any pecuniary reward. His only object, he assured me, was to thwart a plot of the most hellish kind. His next visit was more prolonged than the first, and I elicited from him a promise, given with feigned reluctance, to undertake the task of running the conspirators to earth. Though he was a linguist, the interview ended by my telling him in the plainest of Saxon words that he was a fraud and a swindler. The bomb, which was his stock-in-trade, I impounded; and I afterwards placed it in the Museum at Scotland Yard, where I suppose it still lies.

The notorious "confidence trick" is a fraud which exemplifies in a striking way the truth of my thesis that it is due to their love of filthy lucre that people fall so easily a prey to swindlers. Frederick Williamson, who was head of the detective branch of the Metropolitan Police before the C.I.D. was organised, used to say that the victim of that swindle always intends to defraud the seemingly guileless philanthropist who robs him. And he used also to comment on the fact that the dupe is in so many cases some Colonial or American visitor who would pride himself on being "cute." The details of the game vary according to circumstances, for these swindlers have a keen knowledge of human nature; and it may be played out in an hour or it may last a couple of days; but in its main outlines it is always the same.

The criminals—there must be two in the plot—select their victim, and one of them gets into conversation with him by courteously asking his way, or otherwise. Within half an hour, or it may be next day, they are visiting some public place together—the British Museum is a favourite resort—or they are fraternising at some restaurant or fashionable drinking-bar. Sooner or later the accomplice joins them. To him the first thief discloses the fact that a large sum of money has been left to him for distribution in charity, and his business here is to discharge the trust. But, being a stranger, he is at a loss to know to whom he should apply for help. The accomplice magnanimously offers to undertake the duty. Most gratifying this: but he would not feel justified in handing over the money to a single individual; and, moreover, he very delicately hints that the accomplice is a stranger to him. "But would not your friend join in the trust?" the accomplice asks. This elicits that the friend is also a stranger to him. But if they both can satisfy him that they are men of substance he will gladly avail himself of their services. The accomplice at once produces a sheaf of flash bank notes. The victim follows suit by disclosing the contents of his pocket-book, or else he pleads that he can soon obtain the money.

It is but natural, however, that such a philanthropist should hesitate to trust two gentlemen who are strangers to him, unless they will in some way reciprocate his confidence. The accomplice eagerly responds. He hands over the contents of his pocket-book, and begs the others to leave him, declaring that he will confidently await their return. They act upon his word, and within half an hour they come back and restore his money. How then can the victim refuse to give a similar proof of confidence in the philanthropist? Accordingly he hands over all the cash provided to pay for his visit to Europe, and with this the thieves clear out; and, like Noah's raven, they never return. This is the confidence trick. It has been worked successfully hundreds of times, and it will be worked hundreds of times in the future; and yet one might suppose that no one fit to travel alone could be duped by it.

The "Spanish prisoner" fraud is another hardy annual of the same type. As I was enjoying my arm-chair by the fire after eleven o'clock one night, a young doctor friend of mine arrived, introducing a "pal" of his who wanted me to find him a pensioned officer of my department to assist him on a somewhat delicate mission. After I had given him the name of the man I recommended, my friend urged him to take me into his confidence and tell me his story. His brother-in-law, who was then abroad, had received a letter which, with the connivance of a priest, had been smuggled out of a Spanish prison. The prisoner was a revolutionist, and he had been dispatched to England with a large sum of money—some £30,000—to purchase arms for the conspirators. Before he had time to fulfil his mission, news that his wife was dying compelled him to make a sudden return to Spain, and he had been arrested on a political charge. Being a stranger in England, and knowing no one to whose care he could entrust his money, he had buried it in a field belonging to the gentleman to whom he addressed his letter. He had made such a plan of the place as would enable him to recover it at any time, but this document was in a portmanteau which, in common with all his personal effects, had been seized by his creditors. Two hundred pounds would suffice to discharge all his obligations, and if this amount were granted him he would hand over the field-plan to his benefactor, who could then repay himself tenfold with the buried gold.

That, said my visitor, was the whole story; and his brother-in-law had decided to advance the £200, and had commissioned him to arrange the matter with the priest, whose name and address the prisoner had sent him. "You have not told me the whole story," I replied; "you have kept back everything about the prisoner's lovely daughter; have you got her photograph in your pocket?" My visitor blushed, but he protested that the daughter element was quite incidental, and that, as he had express directions to go to Spain and negotiate the matter, he was bound to do so. In spite of my emphatic warning that the whole affair was a swindle, he fulfilled his commission.

I afterwards learned the result. At the address given, he found not only the priest, but the prisoner himself, who, by an extraordinary chance, had just obtained his release. The money was paid over, and an appointment made for that same afternoon, when the precious plan would be handed to him. A few hours later, however, the visitor received a telegram from the man to say the Police were again upon his track, and he was bolting to France. He would be found, however, at a certain hotel in the French town he named.

I need scarcely add that the visitor never saw

any more either of the prisoner or of the £200. It was a somewhat elaborate phase of a well-known fraud. The poor Spanish prisoner cares little for himself or his buried gold. His only anxiety is to find a safe and happy home for his lovely daughter, now deprived of a mother's care. If the kind English gentleman to whom he entrusts his secret will adopt her as a member of his home circle, and settle one moiety of the gold on her, he may keep the other moiety for himself. This is the bait. The daughter's photograph indicates that she is a real beauty. How can the dupe do better for his son than to make him marry the girl, and thus keep the whole £30,000 in the family?

"The gold brick" is another swindle of the same type. "In vain is the net spread in the sight of any bird." But with human birds the lust of gold is so strong that they will sometimes walk into the net in spite of the plainest warning. In one instance a widow lady of my acquaintance was very indignant because I impounded her correspondence in a gold-brick case, and thus prevented her being duped.

The fraud is a triumph of American ingenuity. A letter is received, addressed to some man whose death has recently been announced, and of course it is opened by his relatives. The writer speaks of his deep and grateful sense of Mr. Blank's kind and generous help at a time when his fortunes were at a low ebb. His long silence has been due to his unwillingness to write until he was in a position to repay the money advanced to him. He is now prepared not only to do this, but to reward his kind benefactor tenfold ; for in "prospecting" he had struck gold, and he wishes him to share his good fortune.

The letter is answered by the dead man's relatives, or by the family lawyer, saying, of course, that the deceased never mentioned the writer's name, and that his papers contain no reference to him. This brings a gushing rejoinder expressing the joy it would give the writer to be able to do a service to the relatives of his benefactor. A few hundred pounds would suffice to buy land that is worth tens of thousands, and if they will send a shrewd and trustworthy man to meet him in New York, he will put the whole matter before him and submit a sample of the ore. Such a matter obviously needs to be dealt with promptly and secretly. The agent crosses the Atlantic ; the swindler talks him over, his stock-in-trade being a cleverly manufactured bit of brick seamed with genuine gold. It is a case of losing a sprat to catch a salmon.

The money is paid, and the dupes wait in vain for news of the gold mine.

This is the simplest and crudest phase of a fraud that is often practised on a much higher and more elaborate scale. As lately as February last the American newspapers reported the conviction of an individual who was said to have amassed a fortune by fleecing the heirs of rich Englishmen in this way. The judge, who sentenced him to a long term of imprisonment, said that he had been preying on the public for forty years, while ostensibly leading a respectable life.

Although betting and gambling cannot be classed as crimes of the type I have been describing, they may not unfitly claim notice in connection with them. According to the city edition of the Bible, the want of money is the root of all evil. But the apostolic *dictum* is that "the love of money is a root of all kinds of evil." And gambling—a vice that springs from an illegitimate craving for money—does as much as drink to corrupt its votaries. Among the legacies left me by my predecessor as head of the C.I.D. was a charge to wage war on "gaming-houses," and I accepted the charge *con amore.*

Gambling Clubs in London

One result of the demoralisation of the Department, described in a preceding article, was an abnormal growth of gambling clubs in London. There were West End clubs frequented by "swells," middle-class clubs run by "snobs," and houses for folk of a lower class in the social scale. I determined to begin at the top, for though the lower-class clubs were far the most mischievous, I was not going to incur the taunt of chevying humble folk and leaving the "toffs" alone. So I held my hand until I was ready to raid the most fashionable club of the kind in London—a house in Park Place, St. James's.

The door of a gaming-house does not stand open, and of course a stranger has no chance of admittance. And yet it was essential that the Police should get in unnoticed, otherwise every outward sign of gaming would be cleared away, and evidence on which to base a charge would fail. But my Inspector in the C Division was a man of exceptional fitness for such work; and on the appointed night he found himself in the middle of the gamblers before any one of them "spied a stranger." The necessary evidence being thus obtained, every person present had to appear before a magistrate. And if the Bar and Club gossip of that day may be trusted, during the few minutes necessarily spent in preparing for the raid, two men passed out whose arrest would have added to the gaiety of nations.

The success of this coup surpassed my expectations; and no club of the same calibre has ever since existed in London. The indignation of the members, of course, was great. Several of them called at Scotland Yard in order to make terms with me, or at least to "draw" me. But all they could get was a declaration of my intention to enforce the law. The first ruse they attempted was to take a private house in the name of a lady of title, and to arrange a weekly meeting there for gambling. I adopted new tactics, and instead of maintaining secrecy, I announced my intention of raiding the place, and the scheme collapsed at once. We then went for the minor clubs scattered throughout London, and one after another was successfully raided by the Police.

My surprise equalled my satisfaction at discovering that my subordinates were as keen as I was myself in this work. Though men of the world, all of them, with broad views of life, such was their estimate of the debasing influence of betting and gambling that any officer who was known to be addicted to these vices was shunned. And as his colleagues refused to work with him, he was soon elbowed out of the Department. A drinking man may possibly be trustworthy when sober; but, drunk or sober, a gambler can never be trusted.

And betting is akin to duelling, but more degrading. Indeed, there was something to be said for the duel in the rough days now past. Webster's Dictionary defines a blackguard as "a person accustomed to use scurrilous language, or to treat others with foul abuse." No gentleman would notice abuse from a fellow of low degree, but if we could imagine a man in a high official position sinking to such a level, the fear of having to face a pistol at twenty paces might restrain his scurrilous tongue. But no defence of this kind can be made for betting. And while the losers of the grand stand do not leave their families to starve, nor take to crime to replenish their purses, these are the results of losses incurred by the crowd upon the course. The time will come when taking another man's money in this way will be deemed disgraceful.

But it was not considerations of this kind that influenced me in the line I took in dealing with the clubs. The design of the State, as Spinoza has aptly expressed it, is to permit every one to live in security—to preserve inviolate his right to live without being injured himself, or doing injury to others. But while keeping this principle in view, the police need not trouble themselves about people who are able to take care of themselves, unless in injuring themselves they do harm to others. And yet to raid low-class clubs while leaving rich men's clubs in peace would be a public scandal.

In another sphere also I always acted on this principle. The police are not the guardians of public morals; and if men whose years and circumstances are such as to indicate that it is only for their own consumption that they obtain evil literature of a certain sort, the Police may well leave them to a higher judgment than the police-court. The reason this unsavoury subject connects itself in my mind with the gambling-curse is that the Post Office is the recognised agency for the dissemination of all such evil wares. In the United States of America any person who uses the "mails" for the furtherance of a fraudulent or illegitimate purpose may be summarily deprived of the use of the Post Office altogether. But in this stupid country of ours the Post Office is bound to accept and transmit anything and everything which outwardly conforms to its rules, unless by a warrant, issued *ad hoc*, the Secretary of State intervenes.

A Purveyor of Literary Filth

I was amazed and distressed at the obstinacy with which my valued friend, Sir Stevenson Blackwood, adhered to the merest technicalities in this matter. Though a righteous man, and devout withal, he was such a hopeless slave to red tape that I appealed to him in vain, first privately, and then in official correspondence, both directly and through the Home Office, to help me in my crusade against the evil to which I allude. But the advent of Sir Spencer Walpole, his successor in office, brought a happy change.

At that time I had succeeded by delicate Police attentions in driving away a notorious purveyor of literary filth. But the man moved his business to Boulogne, and at intervals he crossed the Channel with a portmanteau full of his wares in packets addressed to his clients in this country, and these he posted in Folkestone. I had thus gained nothing by my action; for in Blackwood's time the Police were treated like the man in the street in such matters. But Walpole was a sensible man of the world; and when the Secretary of State summoned him and me to a conference on the matter, he at once declared that whatever was needed to stop such a scandalous abuse of the Post Office should certainly be done.

As everything entrusted to the Post Office is, while in transit, the property of the Crown, the Secretary of State is empowered to give orders respecting the disposal of it. All that was necessary, therefore, in the case above mentioned was that the Folkestone postmaster should be put in touch with the Police, and have orders to send a report to St. Martin's-le-Grand, giving particulars of the packets posted by the criminal, and then to delay their transmission pending instructions. This being arranged, the Police watched for the man, tracked him to the post-office, and arrested him as soon as he had posted his filth. The Secretary of State then issued a warrant directing that the packets should be given up and used as evidence. The case was thus complete, and a conviction followed as of course.

As regards the practical question of the exercise of these powers by the Home Office, I can speak with adequate knowledge. For during the many eventful years that I had charge of Secret Service work at Whitehall, under different Administrations and five successive Secretaries of State, every warrant of this character was prepared by my own hand; and I had always a full cognisance, and often the direction, of the action taken upon it. And I can aver that no such warrants were ever issued save to check serious crime, or to prevent a flagrant abuse of the Post Office, such as I have described. If the facts were generally known, so far from there being even a prejudice against the exercise of such powers, there would be a general outcry against the laxity of Government in this matter. The Post Office is the regular agency for the dissemination of what is fraudulent and corrupting—a state of things which, as I have already said, is not tolerated in America.

CHAPTER XVI

Our British Police System, and its success—The Police are "the servants of the public": this is peculiar to Great Britain—Reforms in Criminology —"Fitting the punishment to the crime"—The "humanitarians"—The amity between all classes in this country—The contrast between London and Paris in this respect—White Lodge and "Prince Eddy"—The influence of the Bible on national life and character—Queen Victoria's first visit to Ireland—Appointment to C.B. and an investiture at Windsor—Appointment to K.C.B.—Reasons for retiring from the public service.

In a previous chapter I noticed briefly the organisation of the Metropolitan Police, as being the best exponent of the system on which Sir Robert Peel remodelled our Police Forces. And in this closing chapter I would notice with equal brevity one of the general causes to which the success of that system is due. I refer to the relations existing between Police officers and the public in this country.

In other lands the Police are regarded only as

representing the Executive Government, whereas with us they belong to the people. And as a result of this, our Police are always ready to help the citizens, and can always count upon receiving help from them in return. Language is supposed to be subordinate to thought, whereas in fact our thoughts are usually influenced, and not infrequently controlled, by words. If, for example, we aver that the Police are the servants of the public, we may seem to be uttering a platitude, whereas we are really giving expression to a conception that is a peculiar characteristic of our national life. For other languages possess no word that is the precise equivalent of "servant" in the phrase in question. And if the conception existed the word would be there also.

No thoughtful person can fail to appreciate the influence of such a conception upon the various relationships of life. And its threatened destruction by the socialism and socialistic trade-unionism of the day is a national danger. The employés of our great railway companies, for example, are as really the servants of the public as are the officers of our Police Forces, and with such men a strike could be justified only in circumstances which in a higher sphere would justify a civil war. This may seem to be a mere digression, but it suggests the explanation of the strange and interesting fact that in the United States no such amity exists between the Police officer and the citizen as that which happily prevails with us.[1] For while the Americans ostensibly share our language, the word "servant" has lost with them the special meaning it has with us. Ultra democratic theories of equality destroy not a little of the benefits which equality is supposed to ensure.

The value of sympathy between the Police and the public declares itself in every sphere of Police duty; but in no way does it attract so much public notice as in the regulation of traffic and the management of crowds. For with us Police orders are regarded, not as directing what the people must do, but rather as intimating what they ought to do. And therefore such orders are enforced without violence and obeyed without resentment. And if this element be important in the maintenance of public order, its value is inestimable in relation to the other main branch of Police duty—the prevention and detection of crime. To its influence is largely due the fact, noticed on a previous page, that in our great cities life and property are safer than in any other country.

But though our criminal statistics will compare favourably with those of our neighbours, they disclose an amount of crime which is distressing and discreditable. This is largely due, however, not to national vice, but to the effect of unwise laws unwisely administered. And drastic reforms in both spheres, such as would command the approval of all thoughtful people, would soon reduce our prison population, and immensely lessen the pecuniary cost of the nation's crime. In recent years much that is valuable has been achieved both in legislation and in administration. And if well-intentioned reforms fail to produce the results expected of them, it is partly because, instead of being framed upon intelligent principles, they are generally a concession to popular sentiment. We need to shake free once for all from the stupid and cruel punishment-of-crime system —an evil legacy from the pagan codes on which our law is based—and to recognise that punishment is merely a means to an end, and that the great end to be kept in view is the protection of the community. And this being so, the proper function of a criminal court is to deal with the offender in whatever way the interests of the community require. Any one, therefore, who plans and perpetrates a crime deliberately and in cold blood should be deemed an outlaw, and deprived of his liberty, not for a measured term, but indefinitely, until he can be released without danger to society.

The only way in which a human tribunal can really "make the punishment fit the crime" is by imposing a punishment of a nature akin to that of the offence. The application of this principle would have a marked effect in checking crimes of violence. But while a criminal has no respect for the sanctity of the person of his victim, we seem to have a morbid respect for the sanctity of the person of the culprit. This indeed is now pressed to such lengths that, as imprisonment is clearly undesirable for youthful offenders, it is proposed that, instead of punishing them, they should be afforded advantages of a kind that the State does not provide for youths who behave themselves. Most people would think that in many cases mischievous lads should be dismissed with a birching. But although this is the treatment accorded to a "Duke's son" at Eton or Harrow, the skin of a "cook's son" is deemed sacred.

And the same principle of adapting penalties to crimes might be applied with marked effect in regard to offences against property. When a thief steals a purse or a teapot it may be right to imprison him for so many months or years. But if nobody laughs when a judge describes this as "fitting the punishment to the sin" it is proof that people have no sense of humour. For what kinship is there between stealing a teapot and being shut up in gaol? Fitting the penalty to the offence was a distinctive feature of the Divine law of the Theocracy. For under that law the interests of the citizen who incurred loss by a crime received full recognition, and his right to restitution or compensation was enforced against the offender. If this principle were adopted in English law it would go far to put an end to deliberate crimes against property; and the mere fact that in certain cases it would be inoperative is no argument against its application generally.[1]

The interests and rights of the law-abiding ought to be the first care of the State in all legislation respecting crime, whereas, in fact, they are ignored. And while the humanitarians have maudlin tears for the sorrows of the criminals, they seem to have no thought for their victims. This, I may add, is not a class question; for in the majority of crimes against property the sufferers are people by whom the loss incurred, though intrinsically small, is deeply felt.

The friendship which happily exists between

[1] In "Criminals and Crime" (James Nisbet and Co.) I have shown how easily this could be enforced in ordinary cases. Of course a question of this kind can receive only incidental notice here.

our Police Forces and the public is in keeping with the relations which have hitherto existed between all classes of the community in this country. In these respects the contrast between London and Paris is extraordinary. Instead of enlarging on this by way of an essay, I will exemplify it by lapsing again into personal narrative. When I attended the Paris *Congrès Pénitentiaire* of 1895, I explained to the Préfet, on calling to pay my respects to him, that I was present in no official or representative character. But a Police Commissioner has only to visit France in order to discover what an important personage he is! M. Lepine "placed the Police of Paris at my disposal," and I availed myself of his courtesy to see "Paris under the pavement."

One night in particular, which I spent in visiting the common lodging-houses, was a revelation to me. Not in districts where the professional *apache* holds sway, but even in central Paris, I saw strata of the population that amply accounted for the street barricades whenever an *émeute* occurs—men who live as far apart from the *bourgeoisie* by whom they are surrounded, as though they were separated from them by a thousand miles of territory. On entering one of these houses I asked my escort—one of the best-known officers of the *Sureté*—

whether I might not pass up the stairs alone. He begged me to do so. On the first floor I found a large unfurnished room the floor of which was literally covered with sleeping men. Presently one of them awoke, and his exclamation on seeing me roused the mass. They sprang up and glared at me like wild beasts. Though I am not specially timid I quailed before them. I was reminded of what Dr. John Paton, of the New Hebrides, once told me of his experiences in confronting a horde of cannibals. In one minute I should have been, metaphorically speaking, swallowed by these savages, and everything belonging to me would have been distributed among them. But the moment the Police inspector appeared beside me, they all collapsed again upon the floor.

And now for a London scene. When Lord Iveagh (Sir Edward Guinness he then was) made his princely grant to provide better quarters for such folk in the Metropolis, he naturally wished to know what the existing common lodging-houses were like, and I brought him to the East End one night on a visit of inspection. We were accompanied by the trustees of his benefaction—Lord Rowton and my old college friend, Lord Rathmore; and Sir Schomberg Macdonnell also was with us. At a Court function men could not be more punctilious about precedence than were my friends when, on entering the first house we visited, I motioned them to go up the stairs. The honour was clearly with Lord Rowton, and he bravely faced the danger. "Hullo, old chap, what are you doing here?" was the exclamation we heard when he had reached the main room at the top of the staircase. For there was his friend and mine, the late Edward Trotter, who told me that he devoted an evening now and then to visiting the house and chatting with the men. "The fellows like it," was his genial comment on his own words. The denizens of our common lodging-houses shake hands with people who shake hands with Royalty! Such is life in this land of ours. How long it is to continue depends upon the Socialists, and upon the neo-Radicalism which truckles to them. And the fact that the first "Royal progress" of the new reign was a visit to the London Hospital gives fresh proof that it is not in this vicarious way only that the poor are in touch with the Palace. This sort of neighbourliness, which smooths away everything that is harmful in class distinction, is a characteristic feature of our national life.

An interesting experience in 1894 impressed this upon me in a striking way. I returned to

London in August after a pleasant three weeks' holiday in the Western Highlands of Scotland —a holiday during which I was so busy idling that I had no time even to read the newspapers. And on the very day of my return I received privately a letter telling me of things that were being said in the Anarchist clubs about "Prince Eddy," as the letter called him, who was then at White Lodge during the absence abroad of the Duke and Duchess of Teck and the Duke and Duchess of York. On riding out to Richmond Park next morning I ascertained that the *ménage* at the Lodge was in all respects like that of a country house when "the family are away"; and the nurse might be seen any day walking unattended in the Park, with her baby charge in her arms. What a delightful picture of the peace and security of life in this favoured land!

On explaining the object of my visit to the lady in charge at White Lodge, I received her cordial consent to certain Police measures which it seemed desirable to adopt. My fear was lest these measures should be talked about and attract notice in the newspapers, as this could not fail to annoy and alarm their Royal Highnesses. But happily this was averted. My visits to the Lodge passed as visits of friendship to the lady in charge; and the nurse, who was taken into our confidence, gladly fell in with our arrangements, and was always keenly appreciative of my unfeigned admiration for "her precious charge," as she called him.

When the Duke and Duchess of Teck returned to England I wrote to say I should do myself the honour of calling to explain my action, and on the 26th of September I had my last ride to White Lodge. Princess Mary received me most graciously, and expressed her gratitude instead of taking me to task for my interference. And I was plied with questions respecting the care of the baby Prince on the return of the Duke and Duchess of York to their residence at St. James's Palace. That was a matter, I said, on which I could not speak: it must be dealt with by the Secretary of State and the Chief Commissioner. But had I not been dealing with it during the last three weeks? Yes, but the circumstances were so exceptional that I had taken the liberty of acting to some extent as an *amicus*. That was precisely what her Royal Highness wished: would I speak to her freely on the subject? And so I found myself discussing what might or might not be done respecting the infant Prince's daily outings. Appeals were made to me to withdraw my objection to the nurse's taking him into the Green Park for his daily airing. Surely no one would hurt the child? But I pleaded that while even the humblest of our own people would act as a body-guard to protect any member of the Royal family, we had to take account of the presence of foreign Anarchists who are criminal outlaws.

As I rode back to town that day I thought much of the proof all this afforded of the relations existing between the Palace and the People. Happy England! Was there another capital in all Europe in which the suggestion would be entertained that an infant Prince in the direct line of succession to the throne might be daily carried by its nurse in the public park?[1]

What explanation can be given of the fact that such friendly relations bind together all classes of the community, from Princes of the Blood to the poorest of the people? It is a national tradition, we shall be told. No doubt; but how is such a tradition to be accounted for? It must be due to some cause which, if not peculiar to Great Britain, has operated here with peculiar force. The cause, moreover, must be adequate to the effects; and therefore to talk of the Anglo-Saxon race, or

[1] This was the last time I ever saw the Princess Mary. But that day thirteen months afterwards—the day before her death—I received a kind message from her Royal Highness.

the climate, or our insular position, would be absurd. Only one such cause can be suggested. A process of negative induction will point us to the influence of the Bible in moulding our national life and character. For in a wholly peculiar sense and degree we have been for centuries "the people of the Book."[1] And this conclusion receives striking confirmation from the fact that present-day tendencies to class hatred and class war have developed side by side with a movement to disparage the Bible, and to dethrone it from the place it has held for so many generations in the estimation of the British people.

The foregoing references to Royalty bring up memories of the first and last occasions on which I came in any special way under Royal notice. And, lapsing once again into my anecdotage, I will give rein to my pen respecting them. When Queen Victoria first visited Ireland, my father was a member of the Dublin Corporation—for in those days the Corporation was composed of

[1] "The power of the book over the mass of Englishmen showed itself in a thousand ways. . . . Far greater than its effect on literature or social phrase was the effect of the Bible on the character of the people at large. . . . The whole moral effect which is produced nowadays by the religious newspaper, the tract, the essay, the missionary sermon, was then produced by the Bible alone; and its effect in this way, however dispassionately we examine it, was simply amazing" (Green's "History of the English People," Book VII. ch. i.).

prominent citizens—and he smuggled me in under the folds of his gown to witness the presentation of the municipal address. I was but a very small child, and I may mention that at that stage of my life my chief grievance was my mother's refusal to allow me to be shorn of ringlets that covered my neck, giving me the appearance of a girl in boy's clothes. Ireland was not used to State functions in those days, and at a critical juncture the mounted escort got out of hand and encroached on the ground occupied by the municipal dignitaries. For the moment confusion reigned. I was driven from my hiding-place into the open, and finding myself in the public gaze, like the Derby dog at Epsom, to the amusement of everybody I ran across and "took cover" behind the Queen.

The last occasion was nearly half a century later. One of the pleasant surprises of my official life was the receipt on December 28, 1895, of the following autograph letter from the Prime Minister :—

"Dear Mr. Anderson,—It gives me great pleasure to be authorised to inform you that the Queen has been pleased to approve that you should be created a Companion of the Bath on the occasion of the New Year, in recognition of the valuable services which you have rendered the community during your tenure of the office of Assistant Commissioner of Police. And it affords me great satisfaction to be the instrument of making known to you Her Majesty's gracious intention.

"Believe me,
"Yours very truly,
"SALISBURY."

There was no investiture that year till after the Birthday, and when at last the date was settled, my name was overlooked. I called on Sir Albert Woods about it, but he told me that the mistake could not be rectified without submitting my case specially to the Queen, and this he could not do. But he sought to soothe me by the assurance that the omission would in no way delay my receiving the decoration. To which I made answer, not without some heat, that its value in my estimation depended on receiving it from Her Majesty in person. Garter was so impressed by my words that he did what he had told me could not be done, and I received a command to lunch at Windsor Castle on the 3rd of July.

The investiture followed the luncheon. And the dearth of ceremony was really an embarrassing element in the function. At Buckingham

Palace the Sovereign is enthroned on such occasions, and one becomes almost an automaton; whereas at Windsor I found the Queen seated in an arm-chair in the middle of the drawing-room. Sir Harry Johnston, who went in immediately before me, told me on coming out that Her Majesty seemed to be annoyed about something or other; and the moment I entered I recognised what he meant. This was not fitted to steady one's nerves, but the cloud passed away before I left the room. When, after placing the decoration on my breast, the Queen gave me her hand, my enthusiastic loyalty and veneration for Her Majesty betrayed me into giving it a real kiss instead of the purely ceremonial touch expected on such occasions, and an amused smile lit up Her Majesty's face as I bowed myself out. But the chagrin I felt at my lapse was entirely relieved when Sir Fleetwood Edwards followed me into the corridor with a hurried, "Anderson, the Queen wants to know something more about you. What shall I say?"[1]

[1] In the following year I was offered another honour, which I declined for somewhat quixotic reasons which I need not mention here; and I have ever since regretted that I did so. On the 20th of September, 1897, I had a visit from M. Goremykine (the Russian Minister of the Interior) and M. Ratchkovsky, to express anew the Tzar's appreciation of the Police arrangements for his safety during his visit. And on the following

After I left office, I received another letter from Lord Salisbury, in which he said: "I am very glad to be authorised to inform you that the King has been pleased to mark his satisfaction at the successful conduct of the duties which you have so lately relinquished, by conferring upon you the rank of a Knight Commander of the Order of the Bath." There was no element of surprise in the pleasure this letter gave me; for two years before the Secretary of State had informed me that this honour awaited me whenever I wished to retire. In his letter to that effect Sir Matthew Ridley went on to say that he would not hear of my resigning at that time, and, indeed, he had no doubt that my term of office would extend beyond his own. And he added that "circumstances" prevented the realisation of his wish to get me the honour at once.

It was not till after my retirement that I discovered what those "circumstances" were—opposition in a quarter to which I should have confidently looked for help in any matter of the kind. But in these closing pages I have no wish to call up painful memories. As the years go by I prefer to dwell upon the many kindnesses and

day M. Ratchkosky called again to offer me the insignia of the Order of St. Anne. I afterwards received a personal token of His Majesty's approval.

benefits received during my official life from men upon whom I had no personal claim. Sir Matthew Ridley himself was of the number ; for I was not a private friend of his. But having been previously Under-Secretary of State, he was aware of the nature and extent of my services to Government in earlier years. And I have since learned that others who shared his knowledge of my work joined in speaking of me both in Downing Street and at the Palace.

I retired when I did for the excellent reason that after forty busy years I felt a strong desire for a more restful life. And, moreover, I had nothing to gain by remaining longer in office. For, as the result of a conference between the Home Office and the Treasury, words had been introduced into an Act of Parliament to secure me a pension at a maximum rate. And in these circumstances, notwithstanding my knowledge of Treasury ways, I could not have imagined that that Department would violate such an arrangement. I had the best legal advice to the effect that I had the law on my side. But had I acted on that advice my chief object in resigning office would have been thwarted ; for litigation is more worrying even than Police work, and the Treasury would have given me plenty of it if I had gone to law to enforce my claim. So I put up with the loss, and banished the matter from my thoughts.

I have already told how, when "in my teens," I relinquished a business career in order to enter Dublin University; and I can still recall the delightful sense of rest and liberty I enjoyed the first day I spent in the quadrangles and park of Trinity College. I was reminded of that experience the day after my retirement from Scotland Yard, when I realised that at last I was free—master of my own time, master of myself!

And now the time has come to lay down my pen and make my bow. The "graver reminiscences" alluded to in my introductory chapter may possibly have some historic interest, and prove of practical value to any who may hereafter be charged with duties such as those with which I was entrusted, first at Dublin Castle and afterwards at Whitehall. But the time for their publication has not arrived. And if this book fulfils the modest promise of its opening page I shall be content.

APPENDIX

In *Blackwood's Magazine* for April, 1910, I made a passing reference to some articles from my pen which appeared in *The Times* in May, 1887, denouncing the American Fenian dynamiters. In reply to a question addressed to him in Parliament on the 11th of that month by Mr. J. Redmond, the Prime Minister said, "If Sir Robert Anderson wrote the *Times* articles, his action was contrary to the rules and traditions of the Civil Service, and, so far as I know, without precedent." *The Times* of the 12th contained the following letter:—

"PARNELLISM AND CRIME.

To the Editor of THE TIMES.

"Sir,—The unfeigned distress I feel at being censured by the Prime Minister, even in a matter so remote as the "Parnellism and Crime" controversy of nearly a quarter of a century ago, is modified by my belief that if I had had an opportunity of laying my case before Mr. Asquith he might have formed a different judgment. The main ground of his censure is that I violated the rules and traditions of the Civil Service. And upon this I should have much to say; but without Mr. Asquith's express permission I will not lay before him what I should offer in my defence.

"But will you allow me to notice the charges implied in Mr. Redmond's question? For the mistake on which it is based I am in part responsible. When drafting my article for this month's *Blackwood*, I told how I once incurred Home Office censure through the smart action of a pressman in the way he reported a historical lecture of mine. And I added, 'To the present hour I do not know whether the Home Secretary was then aware of my authorship of *The Times* articles of May, 1887, on Parnellism and Crime.' But the typist who copied my MS. omitted the 'May'—an omission I never noticed till last Friday. My only connection with that campaign was my three articles entitled 'Behind the Scenes in America.' And a reference to those articles will make two things perfectly clear. First, they were based upon newspaper reports of quasi-public conventions in America, and upon secret Fenian documents proving that those conventions were engineered by the miscreants who promoted the dynamite outrages in this country. And here I may say that not a single statement of mine was ever refuted or even challenged. And secondly, the main purpose with which the articles were written was to thwart that dynamite campaign by letting in the light upon the proceedings of those infamous men.

"My third article leaves no doubt upon this point. The story of the Jubilee dynamite plot is now public property. That plot was hatched at the Chicago Convention of August, 1886, which, as I said, Mr. Redmond attended as Mr. Parnell's representative. But who can point to any word of mine suggesting that Mr. Redmond had any knowledge of the secret sessions of that Convention, or of the secret machinations of the men with whom he was identified on the public platform?

"The secret report of the Convention announced the intention to have 'a pyrotechnic display in honour of the Queen's Jubilee,' or, in other words, as events proved, to bring about a dynamite explosion in Westminster Abbey at the great function of June, 1887. And proofs abounded that this exposure in the columns of *The Times* hindered a plot of far more terrible gravity even than that which was detected and thwarted by police action. Surely this was a public service of such magnitude that in view of it any breach of official propriety might be condoned.

The figment that the Fenian pamphlets I quoted were Home Office papers was fully dealt with in 1889. They were lent to me by my informant, who held them as presiding officer of a Fenian lodge, and his failure to produce them on being called upon to do so would have cost him his life. I would here refer to the letter I addressed to you, Sir, on March 20, 1889. It was only on my own terms that I ever consented to deal with informants. And when Sir William Harcourt once took me to task on this very point I wrote asking him to relieve me of all such duties. His letter in reply is set out on page 18 of my 'Sidelights on the Home Rule Movement.' That book, moreover, plainly indicated my connexion with the 'Behind the Scenes' articles, and

I was definitely told that 'Everybody in Fleet Street knew that I was the author of them.' Hence it was that I referred to them in *Blackwood* in such a matter-of-course and incidental fashion.

"With further reference to Mr. Redmond's question I will only add that for more than a year before I wrote them I had ceased to hold the position which he describes as 'adviser to the Home Office,' and that at no time did the Criminal Investigation Department render any assistance to *The Times* in the Parnell case. I have nothing to conceal in this matter; and if Government will release me from the honourable obligations to reticence respecting the Secret Service work at Whitehall, my defence will be full and complete.

"I am, your obedient servant,

"ROBERT ANDERSON.

"*April* 11, 1910."

My old-fashioned ideas of courtesy and justice led me to assume that this appeal would ensure me a hearing if any action was taken in the matter. But in this I was disappointed; for on April 21st my misdeeds were made the ground of an attack upon me in the House of Commons. I thereupon prepared a full statement of what I had to say in my defence; and this I intended to publish in the present volume. But after the MS. had gone to the printer it was urged upon me that I was thus about to cumber these pages with matter which had entirely ceased to interest the public. Accordingly I recalled it, and decided to content myself with reproducing the above letter to *The Times*, and also the following, which was written twenty-one years ago, when I was attacked upon practically the same grounds as in the debate of last April. Part of it could not be more germane to these recent charges if it were written with special reference to them.

"*To the Editor of* THE TIMES.

"SIR,—It is an excellent rule that Civil servants of the Crown, when publicly attacked, should leave their defence in the hands of their Parliamentary chiefs. I have always observed that rule, and I have no intention of departing from it. But when acts done by me wholly outside the sphere of my official position are assigned as proof that I am unworthy of the office I have the honour to hold under Her Majesty's warrant, I must not shelter myself behind the Secretary of State, for whose generous defence of me in Parliament to-day I am most deeply grateful. It is my privilege, as it is clearly my duty, to put myself right with the public immediately.

"The proper method of doing so is, I admit, by appearing in the witness-box of the Commission Court, and I feel seriously aggrieved that this has been hitherto denied me. As soon as my name was mentioned in the case I asked to be called. For that purpose I saw the Attorney-General on three different occasions, and pressed my wishes upon him and Sir Henry James with a good deal of warmth and pertinacity. And when Sir R. Webster announced what has been called 'the closing of the *Times*' case,' I communicated with him again and received a renewed assurance that my position as a witness was entirely unchanged.

"If I am right in thinking that this whole discussion is grossly disrespectful to the Court over which Sir James Hannen presides, I must plead that I am forced against my will to make myself a party to the 'contempt.'

"I have already intimated that my action in relation to Major Le Caron's evidence was wholly apart from my official position as Assistant Commissioner of Police. It arose from the fact that in former years, in an entirely unofficial position, I rendered advice and assistance to the 1880 Government in matters relating to political crime. A complete explanation of my conduct would involve such an appeal to documents and details as would amount to a disclosure of the Secret Service arrangements of that period. To me, personally, the disclosure would be intensely gratifying. It would, moreover, supply a missing chapter of uncommon interest in the political history of recent years. But Sir W. Harcourt knows me well enough to feel assured that I would not, except under compulsion, say anything to embarrass ex-Ministers of the Crown, who admitted me in any measure to their confidence. Whether it is generous of him to take advantage of this in attacking me as he has done I will not discuss. It is not in keeping with the kindness I have hitherto experienced at his hands.

"For the present, at least, I will confine myself to a bare statement of the facts. I think it will suffice to satisfy even Sir W. Harcourt himself that he has wronged me. This statement, be it remembered, I expect to repeat on oath at the Commission Court.

"When Major Le Caron called on me in

December, having been summoned to England by his father's death, he repeated the expression of his desire to give evidence before the Commission. He had written to me several times about this, and I had already tried to dissuade him from it. I found he was under the impression that the 'prosecution,' as he called it, was a Government matter, and that I was personally interested in it. I set him right on both these points. I assured him that 'Scotland Yard' had no part whatever in the conduct of the case—had it been otherwise, the presentation of it would possibly be very different; but that, in fact, I had never received even a hint that Government wished me to assist the *Times*, and I had never been as much as asked a question as to what I knew of the matters involved in the inquiry. I went on to speak of the terrible risks and penalties he would incur by coming forward, and I urged him strongly to reconsider his decision.

"The following week he came back to say his mind was made up. He could not forget, said he, that he was an Englishman; he had gone into the conspiracy solely to serve his country, and now he would see the matter through, and face the consequences. He ended by asking me to communicate with the *Times* on his behalf. This I point-blank refused to do. I told him again that I had had no communications with the *Times* relative to the conduct of the case before the Commission, and that I would not volunteer; all I would promise was to bear his request in mind if I should be applied to.

"This was in December. Next month Mr. MacDonald appealed to me to help him in finding a witness to prove what he called 'the American part of the case.' I believe he has been generous enough to forgive me for the way I received him. If he had come to me in my official capacity, it would, according to the usual and well-established practice of my office, have been my duty to assist him. But he applied to me only as an *amicus* and an expert, and I sought to put him off by raising all kinds of difficulties, and insisting on unreasonable conditions. I need not give details. I mention the matter merely to mark my anxiety to keep Major Le Caron out of Court, and to explain how it was that Mr. Houston came upon the scene. After much discussion I consented to put the witness in communication with some trustworthy person to be nominated by Mr. MacDonald, under certain stringent conditions of secrecy. Next day he came back to tell me he had asked Mr. Houston to undertake the task. The much talked of 'letter of introduction' was simply three lines to say that the bearer was the person I had promised to send.

"And now as to the letters. Major Le Caron's satisfaction with these arrangements was entirely destroyed by my refusal to help him in preparing his statement. He was crestfallen when I told him I could not see him again until the close of the case. He referred to my often-repeated assurance that I treated his letters as unofficial papers, and declared that he was counting on being allowed to see them, and that if this were denied him he could not 'testify' before the Commission. What was I to do? The strictly regular course was, as Sir W. Harcourt says, to refuse to produce them until I received the inevitable subpœna. To me this was a matter of perfect indifference. But the production of these letters would have been a cause of serious embarrassment to ex-Ministers, and it was solely due to my sense of honourable obligations to them —legal obligation there was none—that I adopted the only alternative open to me. Twenty-one years' acquaintance with Major Le Caron had convinced me that he was a man of scrupulous truthfulness and integrity, and I determined to place his documents at his disposal. I shall be blamed by many for my efforts to prevent him from giving evidence, though I had several good and weighty reasons for doing so. But once he decided to go into the witness-box, my duty seemed clear. The question was not whether I should assist *The Times*, but whether I should set myself to thwart the Court. I may here remark that it is not true that I gave these documents either to *The Times* or to Mr. Houston. Neither *The Times* nor Mr. Houston had access to them. Those which were 'handed in' to the Court were merely manuscript copies of American Fenian circulars. Not a single one of the embarrassing letters has been produced, and if their production be now called for, as I presume it will, Sir W. Harcourt has only himself and Sir Charles Russell to blame for it. It was my anxiety to prevent it which led me to the action now complained of.

"The suggestion that I should have pleaded privilege for these manuscripts as being official documents claims notice. I might, of course, have set up such a plea, but the following facts will make it clear that I could not have sustained it without prevaricating to the verge of falsehood. The letters in question do not come within the definition contained in the Official Secrets Bill now before Parliament. They never were on record in a Government office. They were never 'filed' in a public department. I kept them at my private residence. When Sir W. Harcourt once took me to task for acting in this way with reference to my informants, I immediately asked him to relieve me of my share in the Secret Service work of the Home Office. His reply, which now lies before me, reads strangely when compared with his present utterances.

"Nor had I personally, in relation to such matters, any official position of a kind to lend an official character to the documents in question. If sometimes, through over-zeal, I placed myself 'in evidence' in any way, I was reminded that I had no 'official position whatever.' When I asked for a salary from public funds, I was told it was impossible because I had 'no official position.' So entirely unofficial were my relations with the Secretary of State and the Irish Government that no intimation of them was ever given to the head of the department in which I had then recently become a 'Civil servant,' and the most sustained and scrupulous care was taken to conceal from Her Majesty's Treasury the fact that I had any engagements outside that department. But now, because I happen to be in the line of fire between the two front benches in Parliament, it is contended that I had an official position all the time!

"But, it is urged, these letters were paid for by the Government. This is an *ad captandum* argument to which I could give a complete reply if I were relieved from the honourable obligations to reticence which now restrain me. I will only remark that giving back letters to informants is not an uncommon practice. And this discussion may do good if certain parties on both sides of the Atlantic should learn from it that they may give information to Her Majesty's Government, and receive remuneration for doing so, with the certainty that their secret will be as well kept as Le Caron's was, and that, if they like to make the condition, their communications will be treated as strictly unofficial documents and be returned to them at any time they wish to claim them.

"As regards Sir W. Harcourt's criticisms upon the discharge of my official duties my mouth is closed. But I want to emphasise, and I am prepared to substantiate on oath, the fact asserted by Mr. Matthews, that neither the 'Assistant Commissioner of Police' nor the department which he controls has given help to *The Times* in the presentation of their case before the Commission.

"I am, etc.,

"ROBERT ANDERSON.

"*March* 20, 1889."

I have given this letter *in extenso*, lest any one should suppose that my present defence has been framed to suit the exigencies of the moment. My chief assailant at that time was Sir William Harcourt; and in my Irish book I have recorded how generously he accepted my answer to his attack upon me. For though he was sometimes hasty, he was always just; and he allowed me to remind him how definitely the precise question which underlay his charges had been raised when he was Home Secretary. The circumstances were these. On his taking me to task for the independent attitude I assumed in Secret Service work, and especially with reference to Le Caron and my other informants, I made no reply at the moment; but next day I wrote to him explaining fully my position and views, and begging that as he disapproved of them he would relieve me of all such duties. I mentioned that though I had been receiving letters and reports from numerous informants for so many years, not a line in the handwriting of any one of them was filed in the Home Office. This brought me the reply referred to in my *Times* letter. It was as follows:—

"*Private.*

"My dear Anderson,—I am sorry to find from your letter that you think I have not duly appreciated your indefatigable exertions in the disagreeable duty which has fallen to you.

"I assure you that is altogether a mistake, and I pray you to dismiss it from your mind.

"If we differ sometimes as to modes of procedure, that is a thing which must be looked for.

"Pray go on as you have done in your useful work, and you may rely on entire sympathy and support from me. I am always most grateful for your reports and advice.

"Yours truly,

"W. V. Harcourt."

Appendix

Though I decline to notice the sneers and insults indulged in at my expense in the course of the debate of April 21st, it might seem wanting in respect for the Prime Minister not to offer this reply to his indictment of my conduct.

There is only one other point which I find it necessary to notice. During the debate a letter was read from the gentleman who had charge of the Secret Service in 1887, and in that letter he denied that he had had any knowledge of my *Times* disclosures until after the event. He is quite incapable of intentionally swerving from the truth ; and I can only account for his letter by failure of memory. Our intercourse in relation to Secret Service matters at the period in question was characterised, not by official reserve, but by the confidence and freedom of a close and intimate friendship, which lasted until two years later. Our conferences on official matters were not confined to official hours. My diaries remind me of the many evenings I spent at his house, when all our work was discussed in *tête-a-tête* chats, as we sat together after dinner. I told him everything I was doing, frankly and fully, and without reserve ; and neither then, nor at any time, did he express to me disapproval of my denunciation of the dynamiters in *The Times*.

The Gresham Press,

UNWIN BROTHERS, LIMITED,

WOKING AND LONDON.

Lightning Source UK Ltd.
Milton Keynes UK
UKOW04f1914280616

277289UK00021B/592/P

9 781290 472692